H · THEE · & · BE · THY · GUIDE

O · GO · BY · THY · SIDE

EVERYMAN'S LIBRARY
EDITED BY ERNEST RHYS

REFERENCE

A LITERARY AND HISTORICAL ATLAS OF EUROPE

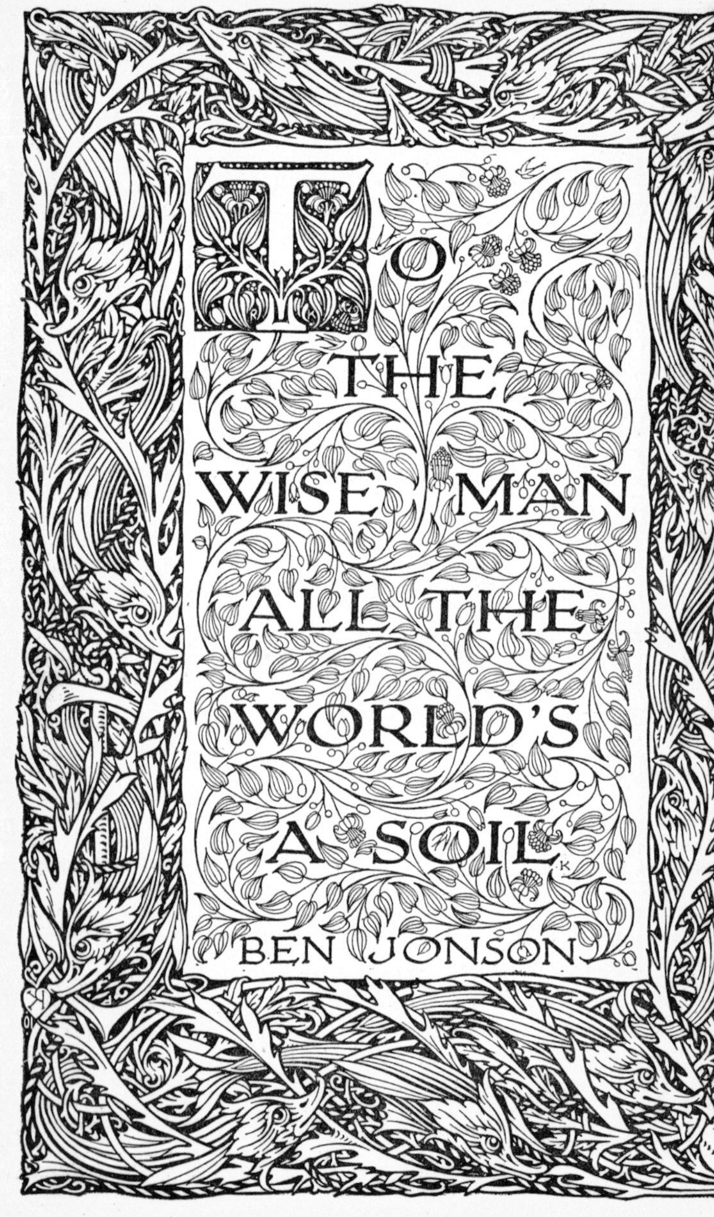
TO THE WISE MAN ALL THE WORLD'S A SOIL
BEN JONSON

A LITERARY & HISTORICAL ATLAS OF EUROPE

J. G. BARTHOLOMEW LL.D

LONDON: PUBLISHED
by J·M·DENT·&·SONS·LTD
AND IN NEW YORK
BY E·P·DUTTON & CO

INTRODUCTION

THIS is the second volume in a set of reference atlases which the publishers have in view for the readers of "Everyman's Library," their object being to provide the literary and historical student with all the necessary geographical data to illustrate the books which he is reading. It was found impossible to give sufficient detail of the whole World in one volume, and it was decided to give an Atlas to each Continent, whose special features could there be adequately treated. Extending the lines of the *Classical Atlas,* this book attempts to cover the geography of Europe, mapped out not only to define the frontiers and countries, but to illustrate history and literature —especially English literature. The changes in the face of Europe that have marked the growth of nations, that went on through the Middle Ages, and have continued to the times of Wellington and Napoleon, the Franco-Prussian War, and to the merging to-day of the military in the industrial struggle, may be followed in the 96 pages of coloured maps which come first in the volume. In addition, some 32 pages of maps in outline will be found covering—

(*a*) The great battles of the world. These are devised with an eye to Creasy's *Fifteen Decisive Battles,* and they go back to classic times; but it will be found that they help to illustrate many modern books too.

(*b*) Maps which relate to English literature. These do not exhaust the field, but they serve as examples of what the student, carrying on the process, may do for himself. By illustrating certain proverbial books and special authors, they show the reader how he may, with the coloured map for his guidance, go on to trace a map to illustrate his own favourite literary region or history-book.

(*c*) An Outline Map of England and Wales showing the situation of the greater monasteries and religious houses.

(*d*) Two extremely interesting Outline Maps which illustrate Mediæval and Revolutionary Paris.

(*e*) The Map of London as it was rebuilt after the Fire, and up to the end of the eighteenth century, must be of very great interest to all readers of Pepys, Evelyn, Johnson, and Goldsmith, and of many other great spirits who haunted these streets, for here are pictured the absolute houses in which Johnson and some of his contemporaries lived.

The small scale of the Map of the Arthurian regions, now for the first time included in an atlas, compels the omission of the local details in each district or region; but the student who shall be tempted by it to make a special map for individual romances, such as Sir Percival, Sir Tristram, or the Twrch Trwyth in the *Mabinogion*, will find in the end that he has gained a new idea of what romance means. The map of the Dickens country, again, covers nearly all the chief places of interest in the novels; but it would require a series of charts to represent each book in detail. One would like to add a Dickens London; but that, any student can make who will profit by example and trace for himself the localities of the different London stories. To do this, he will require, however, a pretty early nineteenth-century map stated in some street-detail.

Another feature which we believe to be quite unique is that we have been able, by the kindness of Mr. Bernard Roth (the eminent orthopædic surgeon), to add a sketch of the English Coinage from 150 B.C. up to King Edward VII.'s time, and to illustrate it with eight pages of examples from his own unique collection. This indeed brings reality into romance, for no longer is Shakespeare's "Cymbeline" a mythical person, but a living king who coined his own coins in his mint at Colchester, and many other dim historic personages stand out vividly when we see their image and superscription upon their own coins. This could only have been possible through the kindness of Mr. Roth, and we owe him our most hearty thanks.

We have to thank Miss Edwardes, too, for the careful compilation of a Gazetteer, drawn up with definite bearing upon local events and historic and literary associations, which, with the maps themselves to lend it reality, helps to make topography alive and human. A few places of note, it may be, are not to be found in the maps, but this is usually because they are mere villages, fields, or roads which it would require a map of an immense scale to contain; but the latitude and longitude in each case is given so that the reader may easily locate the spot.

It is intended to follow this Atlas speedily with one of America, which will be treated on the same lines, and with the same full illustrative detail, and that in turn will be followed by separate atlases of Asia and of Africa and Australia, so that the world's geography and history will be very fully covered when the set is complete.

The publishers would like to say how much they are indebted to the skill and knowledge of Dr. Bartholomew, who has been exceedingly fruitful in suggestion and prodigal to liberality in making new plates whenever any new value could be given to the maps. Indeed, their enterprise would have been impossible, and lacking in many of its most essential features, but for his skilled aid and interest in the venture.

CONTENTS

COLOURED MAPS

LINE MAPS

FIFTEEN DECISIVE BATTLES OF THE WORLD

FAMOUS BRITISH BATTLES

MAPS ILLUSTRATING DISTRICTS CONNECTED WITH FAMOUS BOOKS AND THEIR AUTHORS

THE WORLD ACCORDING TO ORTELIUS, 1570

TYPUS ORBIS TERRARUM

AMERICA SIVE INDIA NOVA

EUROPA

ASIA

AFRICA

MAR DEL ZUR

MAR DEL NORT

OCEANUS AETHIOPICUS

MAR DI INDIA

EL MAR PACIFICO

TERRA AUSTRALIS NONDUM COGNITA

Psitacorum regio

Circulus Arcticus

Tropicus Cancri

Circulus Aequinoctialis

Tropicus Capricorni

Circulus Antarcticus

Nova Guinea

Archipelago di S.Lazaro

Terra del Fuego

Estreche di Magallanes

Rio de la Plata

Brasil

Peru

Chile

Chica

Amazones

Caribana

Florida

Nova Francia

Chilaga

Quivira

Anian

Estotilant

Groclant

Islant

Noruegia

Suedia

Russia

Tartaria

Germania

Gallia

Hispania

Italia

Barbaria

Aegyptus

Nubia

Abissini

Agisymba

Manicongo

Arabia

Persia

Turchestan

Corasan

Guzarare

India orientalis

China

Cathaio

Mongol

Iapan

Philippinas

Mindanao

Burneo

Sumatra

Iava maior

Iava minor

Zeilan

Malacha

Maletur

Lucach

Beach

C.Bonae Spei

Los Romeros

Tristan de Acuna

S.Helena

Ascension

S.Tomas

S.Paulo

Las Acores

La Bermuda

Cuba

Spagnola

Iamaica

Hispania nova

I.di los Tiburones

I.di S.Pedro

Las Boloanes

Abreojo

C.de S.Maria

John Bartholomew & Co., Edinr.

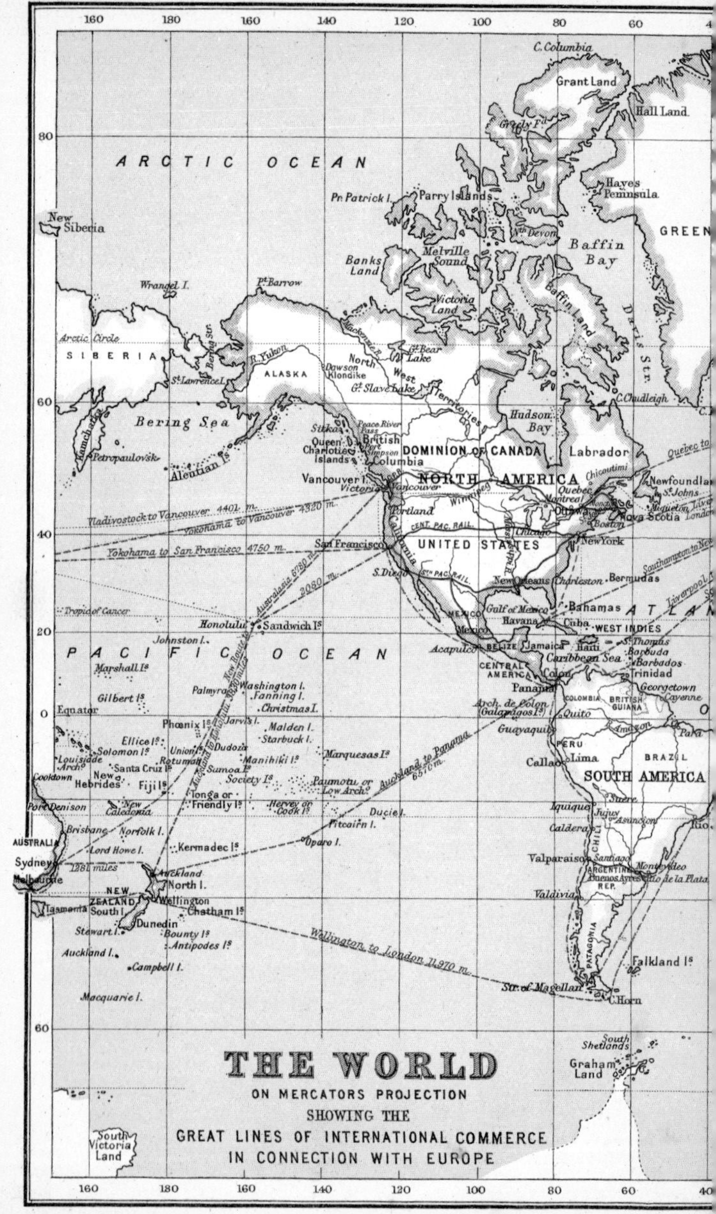
THE WORLD
ON MERCATORS PROJECTION
SHOWING THE
GREAT LINES OF INTERNATIONAL COMMERCE
IN CONNECTION WITH EUROPE
ARCTIC OCEAN
PACIFIC OCEAN
C. Columbia
Grant Land
Hall Land
Grinnell Ld
Hayes Peninsula
Pr Patrick I.
Parry Islands
New Siberia
Nth Devon
Baffin Bay
Melville Sound
Banks Land
Victoria Land
Baffin Land
Davis Str.
Wrangel I.
Pt Barrow
Arctic Circle
SIBERIA
Bering Str.
R. Yukon
ALASKA
Dawson Klondike
Mackenzie R.
Gt Bear Lake
North West Territories
Gt Slave Lake
St Lawrence I.
C. Chudleigh
Bering Sea
Kamchatka
Petropaulovsk
Aleutian Is
Sitka
Queen Charlotte Islands
Peace River Pass
British Columbia
Port Simpson
Hudson Bay
DOMINION OF CANADA
Labrador
Quebec to
Chicoutimi
NORTH AMERICA
Newfoundla
St Johns
Quebec
Vancouver I.
Victoria
Vancouver
Winnipeg
Montreal
Ottawa
Miquelon
Nova Scotia
Portland
Boston
Vladivostock to Vancouver 4401 m.
Yokohama to Vancouver 4320 m.
CENT. PAC. RAIL.
Chicago
San Francisco
UNITED STATES
New York
Yokohama to San Francisco 4750 m.
California
Mississippi R.
Southampton to New
Australasia 6780 m.
2080 m.
S. Diego
STH PAC. RAIL.
New Orleans
Charleston
Bermudas
Liverpool
Tropic of Cancer
Gulf of Mexico
Bahamas
ATLAN
MEXICO
Mexico
Havana
Cuba
Honolulu
Sandwich Is
WEST INDIES
Johnston I.
Acapulco
BELIZE
Jamaica
Haiti
St Thomas
Barbuda
Caribbean Sea
Barbados
Marshall Is
CENTRAL AMERICA
Colon
Trinidad
New Route to
Panama
Georgetown
Palmyra
Washington I.
Fanning I.
Cayenne
Gilbert Is
Arch. de Colon (Galapagos Is)
COLOMBIA
BRITISH GUIANA
Christmas I.
Equator
Quito
Phoenix Is
Jarvis I.
Malden I.
Guayaquil
Amazon
Para
Starbuck I.
Ellice Is
Solomon Is
Union Is
Dudoza
PERU
BRAZIL
Rotumah
Manihiki Is
Marquesas Is
Louisiade Arch.
Santa Cruz Is
Samoa Is
Callao
Lima
Auckland to Panama 6570 m.
Cooktown
New Hebrides
Fiji Is
Society Is
Paumotu or Low Arch.
SOUTH AMERICA
Tonga or Friendly Is
Port Denison
New Caledonia
Hervey or Cook Is
Sucre
Ducie I.
Iquique
Jujuy
Brisbane
Norfolk I.
Pitcairn I.
Asuncion
Caldera
Rio
AUSTRALIA
Oparo I.
CHILI
Lord Howe I.
Kermadec Is
Sydney
Valparaiso
Santiago
1281 miles
Auckland
ARGENTINE REP.
Montevideo
Melbourne
Buenos Ayres
Rio de la Plata
North I.
NEW ZEALAND
Wellington
Valdivia
Tasmania
South I.
Chatham Is
Dunedin
Bounty Is
Stewart I.
Antipodes Is
Wellington to London 11,970 m.
PATAGONIA
Auckland I.
Campbell I.
Falkland Is
Str. of Magellan
C. Horn
Macquarie I.
South Shetlands
Graham Land
South Victoria Land
160
180
140
120
100
80
60
40
20
0

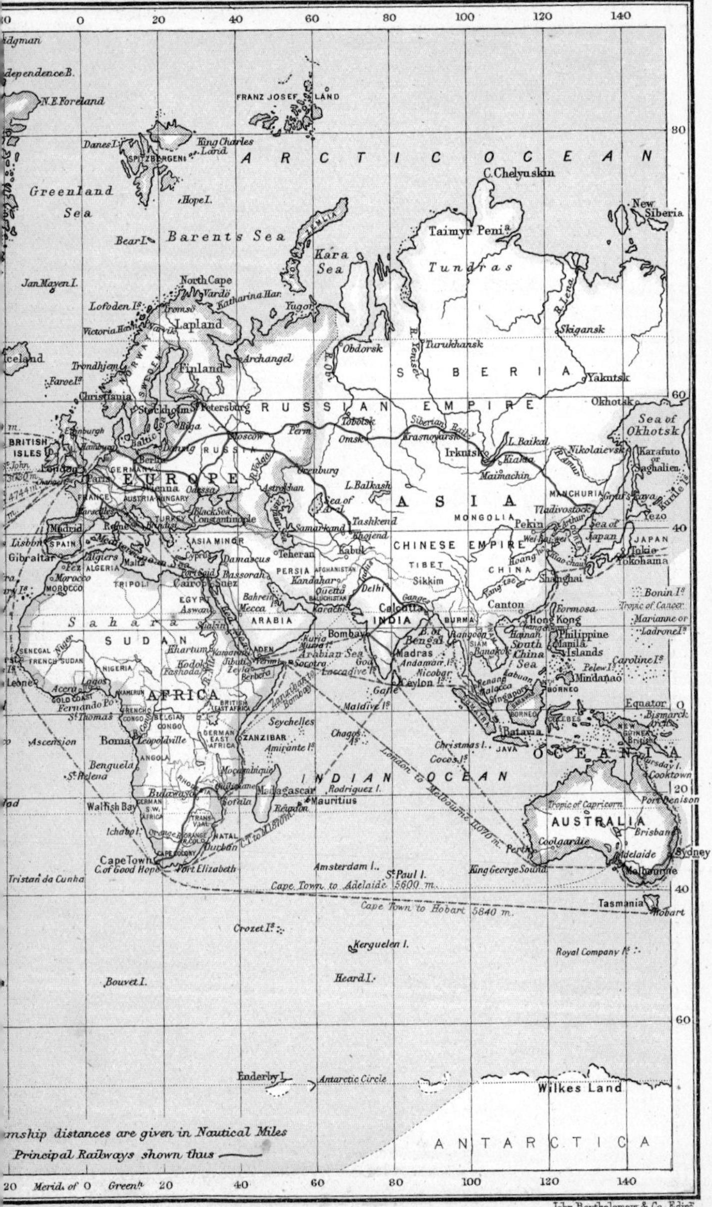

FRANZ JOSEF LAND
N.E. Foreland
Danes I.
SPITZBERGEN
King Charles Land
ARCTIC OCEAN
C. Chelyuskin
Greenland Sea
Hope I.
New Siberia
Bear I.
Barents Sea
NOVAYA ZEMLIA
Taimyr Peni.a
Kara Sea
Tundras
Jan Mayen I.
North Cape
Vardö
Katharina Har.
Lofoden Is.
Tromsö
Yugor
R. Lena
Lapland
Victoria Havn
Narvik
Skigansk
NORWAY
SWEDEN
Obdorsk
R. Obi
R. Yenisei
Turukhansk
Iceland
Archangel
Trondhjem
Finland
SIBERIA
Yakutsk
Faroe Is.
Christiania
Stockholm
Petersburg
RUSSIAN EMPIRE
Okhotsk
Sea of Okhotsk
Edinburgh
Riga
Tobolsk
Siberian Railway
BRITISH ISLES
Moscow
Perm
Omsk
Krasnoyarsk
L. Baikal
Irkutsk
Nikolaievsk
Karafuto or Saghalien
Danzig
RUSSIA
Berlin
Kiakta
R. Amur
London
GERMANY
R. Volga
Orenburg
Maimachin
Paris
EUROPE
Vienna
Odessa
Astrakhan
L. Balkash
MANCHURIA
FRANCE
AUSTRIA-HUNGARY
Caspian Sea
Sea of Aral
ASIA
Vladivostock
Kurile Is.
Marseilles
Black Sea
Yezo
Madrid
Rome
Constantinople
TURKEY
MONGOLIA
Pekin
Sea of Japan
Lisbon
SPAIN
Brindisi
Samarkand
Tashkend
Khojend
JAPAN
Tokio
Yokohama
Gibraltar
Algiers
Malta
ASIA MINOR
Cyprus
Damascus
Teheran
Kabul
CHINESE EMPIRE
Fez
Morocco
MOROCCO
ALGERIA
TRIPOLI
Port Said
Cairo
Suez
Bassorah
PERSIA
AFGHANISTAN
Kandahar
TIBET
CHINA
Shanghai
Quetta
BALUCHISTAN
Sikkim
Yang-tse
Bonin Is.
EGYPT
Aswan
Bahrein Is.
Mecca
Karachi
Delhi
Ganges
Tropic of Cancer
Calcutta
Canton
Formosa
Sahara
ARABIA
INDIA
BURMA
Hong Kong
Marianne or Ladrone Is.
Suakin
Red Sea
SUDAN
Khartum
Bombay
B. of Bengal
Rangoon
Hainan
Philippine Islands
Manila
Kassala
ADEN
Arabian Sea
SIAM
Bangkok
South China Sea
SENEGAL
FRENCH SUDAN
Kodok
Fashoda
Jibuti
Zeyla
Berbera
Perim
Socotra
Goa
Madras
Andaman Is.
Nicobar
Caroline Is.
Pelew Is.
Laccadive Is.
NIGERIA
R. Nile
Ceylon I.
Labuan
Mindanao
Accra
Lagos
KAMERUN
AFRICA
BRITISH EAST AFRICA
Galle
Penang
Malacca
Singapore
BORNEO
GOLD COAST
Fernando Po
St. Thomas
FRENCH CONGO
BELGIAN CONGO
Zanzibar to Bombay
Maldive Is.
SUMATRA
SARAWAK
CELEBES
Equator
Bismarck Arch.
NEW GUINEA
British
Seychelles
Batavia
Boma
Leopoldville
GERMAN EAST AFRICA
ZANZIBAR
Chagos Is.
Ascension
Amirante Is.
Christmas I.
JAVA
OCEANIA
ANGOLA
Cocos Is.
Thursday I.
Cooktown
Benguela
Moçambique
St. Helena
INDIAN OCEAN
London to Melbourne 11070 m.
Madagascar
Rodriguez I.
Port Denison
Bulawayo
Sofala
Mauritius
Tropic of Capricorn
Walfish Bay
GERMAN S.W. AFRICA
Réunion
TRANSVAAL
AUSTRALIA
Brisbane
Ichabo I.
ORANGE R.COLO.
NATAL
Durban
C.T. to M. 11810 m.
Coolgardie
Perth
Adelaide
Sydney
CAPE COLONY
Cape Town
C. of Good Hope
Port Elizabeth
Amsterdam I.
St. Paul I.
King George Sound
Melbourne
Tristan da Cunha
Cape Town to Adelaide 5600 m.
Tasmania
Cape Town to Hobart 5840 m.
Hobart
Crozet Is.
Kerguelen I.
Royal Company Is.
Bouvet I.
Heard I.
Enderby L.
Antarctic Circle
Wilkes Land
ANTARCTICA
...mship distances are given in Nautical Miles
Principal Railways shown thus
Merid. of 0 Greenh.
John Bartholomew & Co., Edinr.

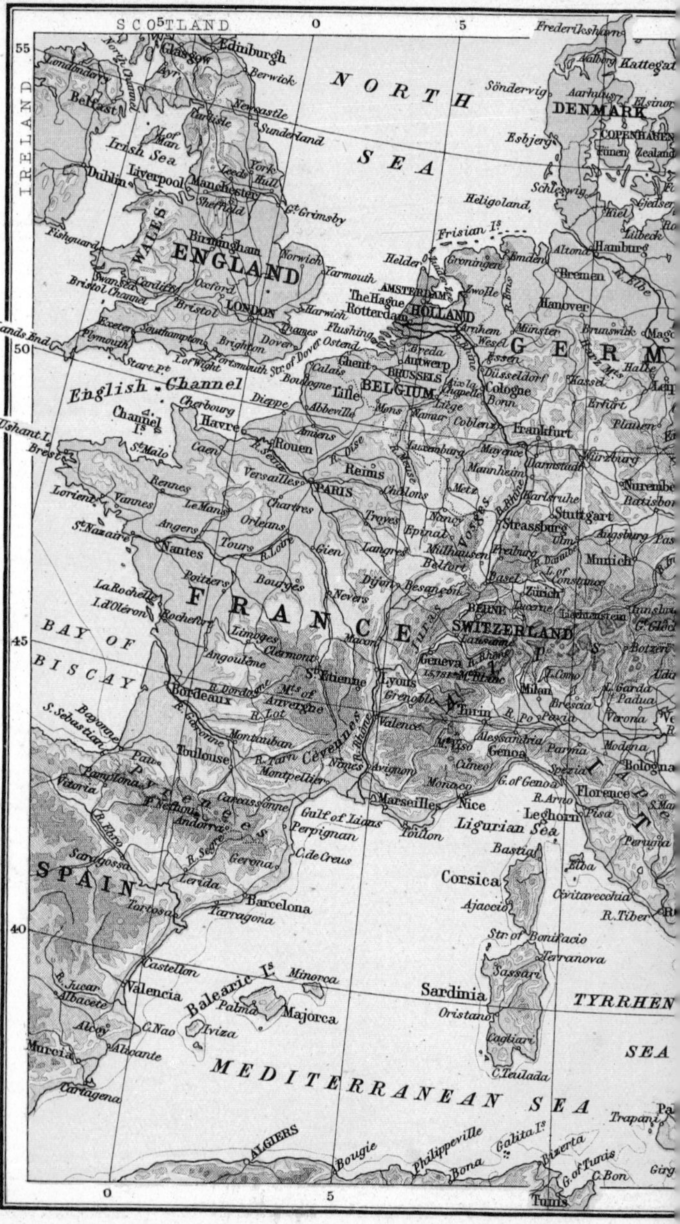

SCOTLAND 5 0 5
Frederikshavn
55
North Channel
Glasgow
Edinburgh
Londonderry
Ayr
Berwick
NORTH
Aalborg
Kattegat
IRELAND
Belfast
Newcastle
Carlisle
Söndervig
Aarhus
Elsinor
DENMARK
I. of Man
Sunderland
Esbjerg
COPENHAGEN
Irish Sea
SEA
Fünen
Zealand
Dublin
Liverpool
Leeds
York
Hull
Manchester
Sheffield
Schleswig
Heligoland
Gt. Grimsby
Kiel
Gjedser
WALES
Fishguard
Lübeck
Frisian Is.
Birmingham
Norwich
Groningen
Emden
Altona
Hamburg
ENGLAND
Helder
Zuider Zee
Bremen
R. Elbe
Swansea
Cardiff
Oxford
Yarmouth
AMSTERDAM
Zwolle
Bristol Channel
The Hague
R. Ems
Hanover
Bristol
LONDON
Rotterdam
HOLLAND
Harwich
Lands End
Exeter
Southampton
Thames
Flushing
Arnhem
Münster
Brunswick
Plymouth
Dover
Ostend
Wesel
Brighton
Str. of Dover
Breda
R. Rhine
GERM
Harz Mts.
50
I. of Wight
Portsmouth
Ghent
Antwerp
Essen
Halle
Start Pt.
Calais
BRUSSELS
Düsseldorf
Kassel
English Channel
Boulogne
BELGIUM
Aix la Chapelle
Cologne
Lille
Liège
Bonn
Erfurt
Cherbourg
Dieppe
Abbeville
Mons
Namur
Channel Is.
Havre
Coblenz
Frankfurt
Plauen
Ushant I.
Amiens
St. Malo
Brest
Caen
Rouen
Luxemburg
Mayence
Darmstadt
Würzburg
R. Seine
R. Oise
R. Meuse
Reims
Mannheim
Versailles
Rennes
PARIS
Lorient
Vannes
Châlons
Metz
Nuremberg
Le Mans
Chartres
Karlsruhe
Ratisbon
R. Rhine
Vosges
Stuttgart
Troyes
Orleans
Angers
Nancy
Strassburg
St. Nazaire
Epinal
Augsburg
Ulm
Tours
Nantes
R. Loire
Gien
Langres
Mülhausen
Freiburg
R. Danube
Munich
Belfort
Poitiers
Bourges
L. of Constance
Basel
Dijon
Besançon
La Rochelle
Zürich
FRANCE
Nevers
I. d'Oléron
BERNE
Lucerne
Liechtenstein
Rochefort
Juras
SWITZERLAND
BAY OF
Limoges
Macon
Lausanne
45
R. Rhone
Angoulême
Clermont
Geneva
BISCAY
15,781 Mt. Blanc
St. Etienne
Lyons
L. Como
Bordeaux
R. Dordogne
Mts. of Auvergne
Milan
L. Garda
Padua
Grenoble
Brescia
S. Sebastian
Bayonne
R. Garonne
R. Lot
Valence
Turin
R. Po
Pavia
Verona
Montauban
Mt. Viso
Alessandria
Parma
Modena
Cévennes
Genoa
Pau
Toulouse
R. Tarn
R. Rhone
Nîmes
Bologna
Montpellier
Avignon
Cuneo
Pyrenees
Pamplona
Vitoria
Spezia
Monaco
G. of Genoa
Carcassonne
Florence
Marseilles
Nice
P. Nethou
R. Arno
Andorra
Leghorn
R. Ebro
Gulf of Lions
Pisa
Perpignan
Toulon
Ligurian Sea
R. Segre
Bastia
Perugia
Saragossa
C. de Creus
Gerona
Elba
Corsica
SPAIN
Lerida
Civitavecchia
Ajaccio
Tortosa
Barcelona
R. Tiber
Tarragona
40
Str. of Bonifacio
Terranova
Castellon
Sassari
Minorca
R. Jucar
Balearic Is.
Valencia
Sardinia
Albacete
TYRRHEN
Palma
Majorca
Oristano
Alcoy
C. Nao
Iviza
Cagliari
SEA
Murcia
Alicante
MEDITERRANEAN SEA
C. Teulada
Cartagena
Trapani
ALGIERS
Philippeville
Galita Is.
Bizerta
Bougie
Bona
G. of Tunis
C. Bon
Tunis
0 5

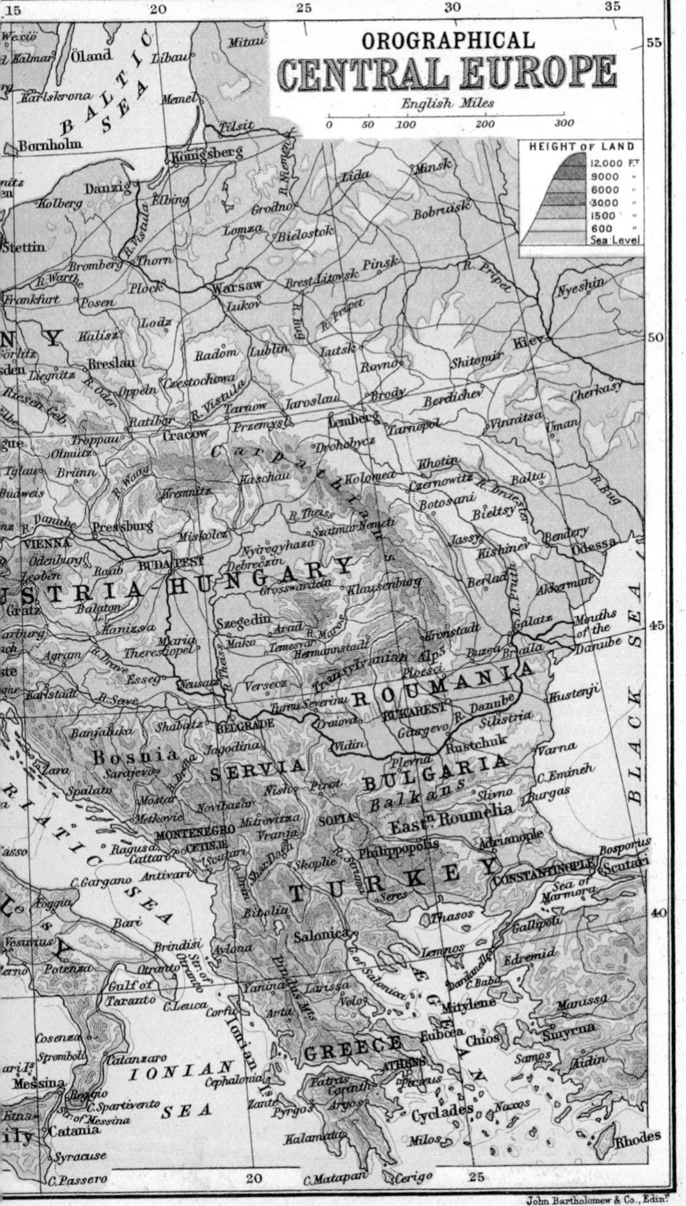

John Bartholomew & Co., Edin.r

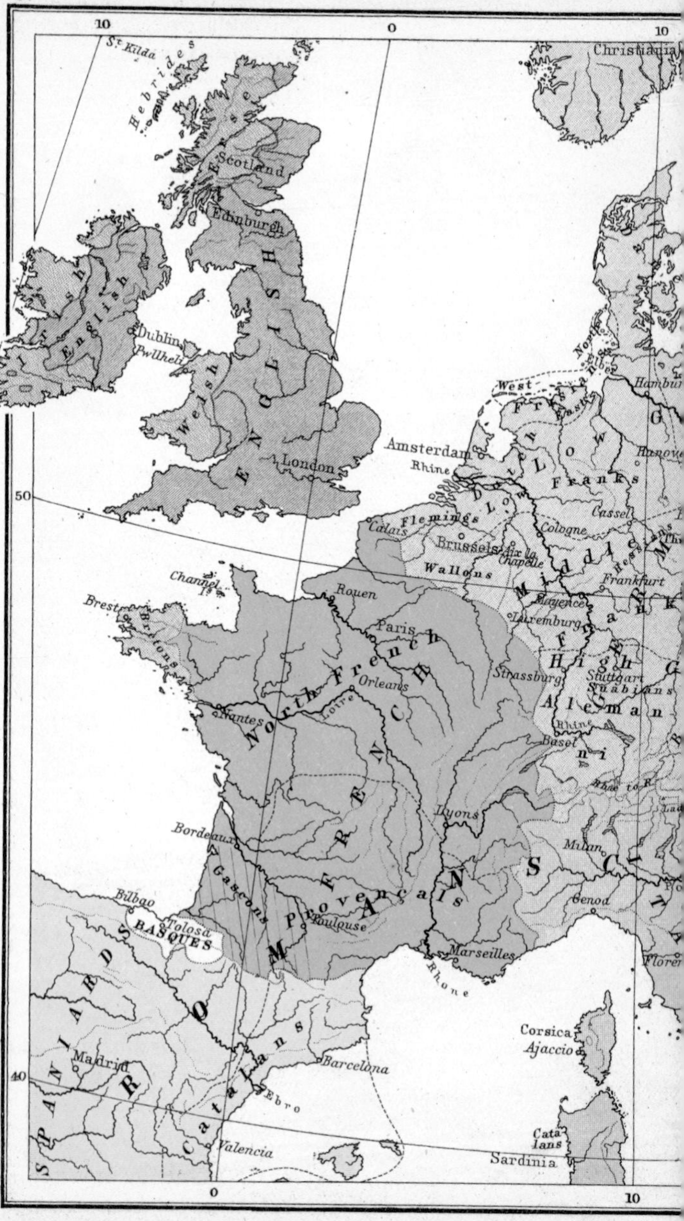

10
0
10
St. Kilda
Hebrides
Christiania
Scotland
Edinburgh
Irish
English
ENGLISH
Dublin
Pwllheli
Welsh
London
Amsterdam
Rhine
North
Elbe
Hamburg
West
Frisians
East
Low
Franks
Hanover
Dutch
Low
Cassel
Calais
Flemings
Brussels
Aix la Chapelle
Cologne
Wallons
Middle
Hessians
Frankfurt
Franks
Mayence
Luxemburg
Channel Is.
Brest
Bretons
Rouen
Paris
North French
Orleans
Nantes
Loire
FRENCH
Strassburg
High
Stuttgart
Suabians
Alemanni
Rhine
Basel
Lyons
Milan
Bordeaux
Gascons
Provençals
Toulouse
ROMANS
Bilbao
Tolosa
BASQUES
SPANIARDS
Madrid
Catalans
Barcelona
Ebro
Valencia
Marseilles
Rhone
Genoa
Corsica
Ajaccio
Cata lans
Sardinia
Florence
50
40
0
10

John Bartholomew & Co., Edin.

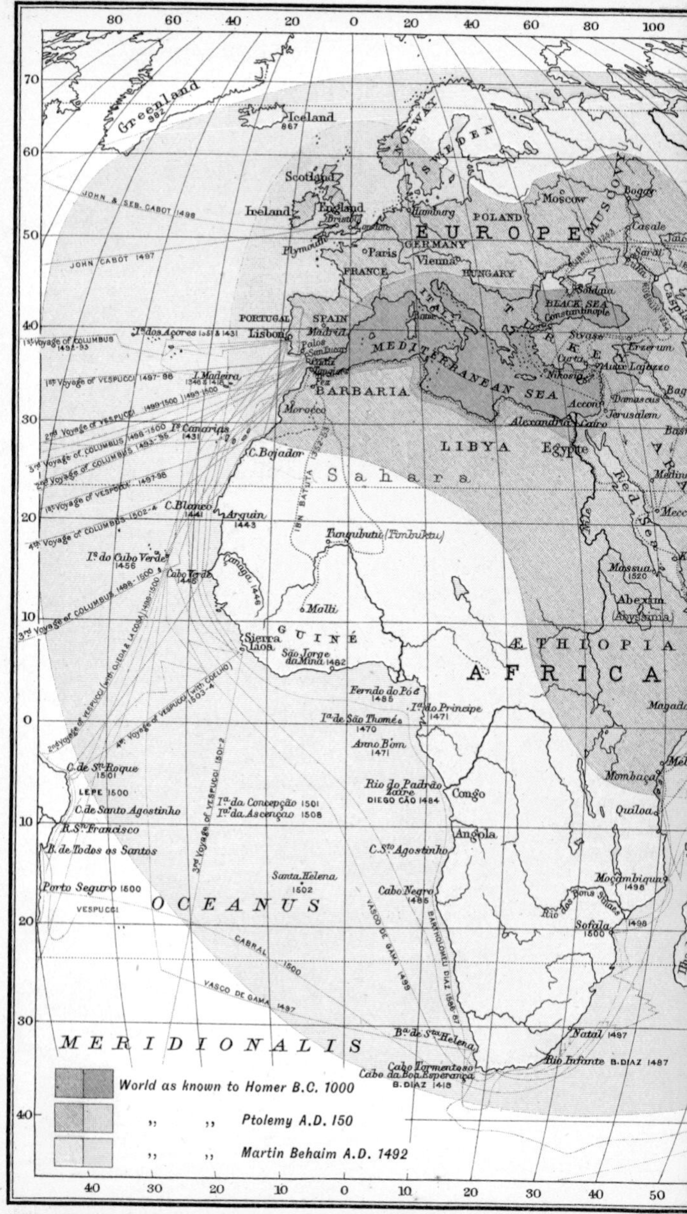
Greenland 982
Iceland 867
NORWAY
SWEDEN
Scotland
Ireland
England
Bristol
London
Plymouth
Hamburg
POLAND
Moscow
MUSCOVY
Bogar
Casale
Saral
EUROPE
GERMANY
Paris
Vienna
FRANCE
HUNGARY
Soldaia
BLACK SEA
Constantinople
ITALY
Rome
PORTUGAL
SPAIN
Lisbon
Madrid
Palos
San Lucar
Cadiz
Tangier
Fez
TURKEY
Sivas
Erzerum
Laiazzo
Nikosia
Accon
Damascus
Jerusalem
MEDITERRANEAN SEA
BARBARIA
Morocco
Alexandria
Cairo
LIBYA
Egypte
C. Bojador
Sahara
IBN BATUTA 1352-53
Red Sea
Nile
Mecca
C. Blanco 1441
Arguin 1443
Tungubutu (Timbuktu)
Massua 1520
Abexim (Abyssinia)
Is. do Cabo Verde 1456
Cabo Verde 1445
Canaga 1446
Malli
Sierra Lioa
GUINÉ
São Jorge da Mina 1482
ÆTHIOPIA
AFRICA
Ferndo do Pó 1485
Ia. do Principe 1471
Ia. de São Thomé 1470
Anno Bom 1471
Magado
Mombaça
Rio do Padrão Zaire
DIEGO CÃO 1484
Congo
Quiloa
Angola
C. Sto. Agostinho
Santa Helena 1502
Cabo Negro 1485
Moçambique 1498
Rio dos Bons Sinaes
Sofala 1500
1498
Natal 1497
Rio Infante B. DIAZ 1487
Ba. de Sta. Helena
Cabo Tormentoso
Cabo da Boa Esperança
B. DIAZ 1418
JOHN & SEB. CABOT 1498
JOHN CABOT 1497
Is. dos Açores 1351 & 1431
1st Voyage of COLUMBUS 1492-93
1st Voyage of VESPUCCI 1497-98
I. Madeira 1346 & 1418
2nd Voyage of VESPUCCI 1499-1500
Is. Canarias 1431
3rd Voyage of COLUMBUS 1498-1500
2nd Voyage of COLUMBUS 1493-96
1st Voyage of VESPUCCI 1497-98
4th Voyage of COLUMBUS 1502-4
3rd Voyage of COLUMBUS 1498-1500
2nd Voyage of VESPUCCI (with OJEDA & LA COSA) 1499-1500
4th Voyage of VESPUCCI (with COELHO) 1503-4
3rd Voyage of VESPUCCI 1501-2
C. de Sto. Roque 1501
LEPE 1500
C. de Santo Agostinho
R. Sto. Francisco
B. de Todos os Santos
Is. da Concepção 1501
Is. da Ascenção 1508
Porto Seguro 1500
VESPUCCI
OCEANUS
MERIDIONALIS
CABRAL 1500
VASCO DE GAMA 1497
VASCO DE GAMA 1499
BARTHOLOMEU DIAZ 1486-87
World as known to Homer B.C. 1000
,, ,, Ptolemy A.D. 150
,, ,, Martin Behaim A.D. 1492
80 60 40 20 0 20 40 60 80 100
70 60 50 40 30 20 10 0 10 20 30 40
40 30 20 10 0 10 20 30 40 50

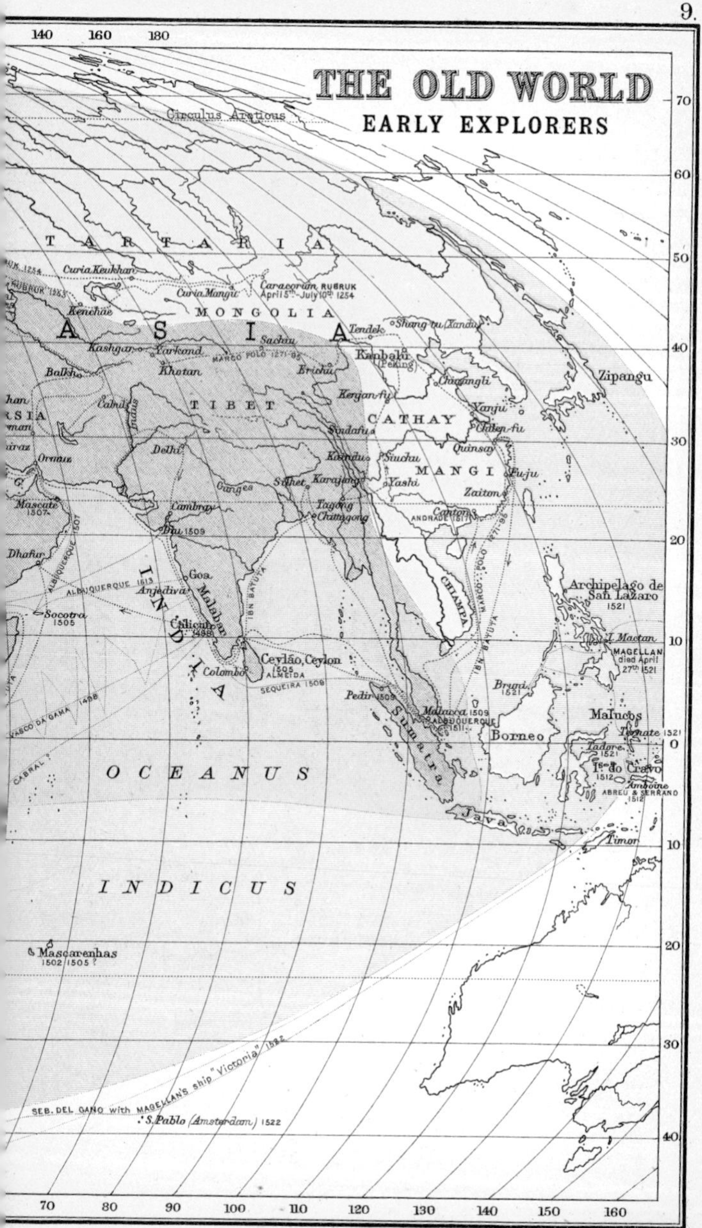

THE OLD WORLD

EARLY EXPLORERS

John Bartholomew & Co., Edinr.

CALEDONIA
Picts
Iona
Scots
HIBERNIA
Anglo Saxons
Eboracum
BRITAIN
Londinium
Jutes
Britons
JUTES
Angles
DANES
Frisians
SAXONS
Salians
Tornacum
Colonia
Rotomagus
Liftinas
Suessiones
Remi
EMPIRE OF THE FRANKS
Riparians
Magontia
THURINGIANS
Armorica
Syagrius
Parisii
Trèves
Wormatia
Alamanni
Mettis
Regina
Aurelianum
Andecavi
Stratisburg
Castra Batava
Andelaus
Divio
Vindonissa
Juvavium
Tiburn
Turones
Bituriges
Augustodunum
BURGUNDIAN KINGDOM
Pictavium
Ecolisma
Arperni
Geneva
Tridentum
Burdigala
Lugdunum
Mediolanum
Verona
Aquileia
Vienna
Ticinum
Venetia
Lucus
SUEVIAN KINGDOM
Pampilona
Pavia
Pollentia
Ravenna
Faventia
Portucale
Bracara
Palentia
Tolosa
Nemausus
Avenio
Arelate
Genua
Pisae
Faesulae
Salamantica
Narbona
Massilia
EMPIRE OF THE OSTROGOTHS
Conimbriga
Caesaraugusta
Ilerda
Gerunda
Perusia
Ulixipona
Segovia
Complutum
EMPIRE OF THE VISI-GOTHS
Dertosa
Barcino
Tarraco
Corsica
Aleria
Centumcellae
Toletum
Roma
Lusitania
Ostia
Segobrica
Turris
Beneventum
Pax
Emerita
Minorica
Neapolis
Oretum
Majorica
Sardinia
Valentia
Corduba
Evusus
EMPIRE OF THE VANDALS
Illiberis
Hispalis
Gades
Caralis
Malaca
Carthago-spartaria
Tingis
Lilybaeum
Sicilia
Cæsarea
Igilgilis
Hippo Zaritus
Agrigentum
Quida
Saldae
Hippo Regius
Carthago
Hadrumentum
Thapsus
English Miles
0 50 100 200 300 400 500

John Bartholomew & Co., Edin^r.

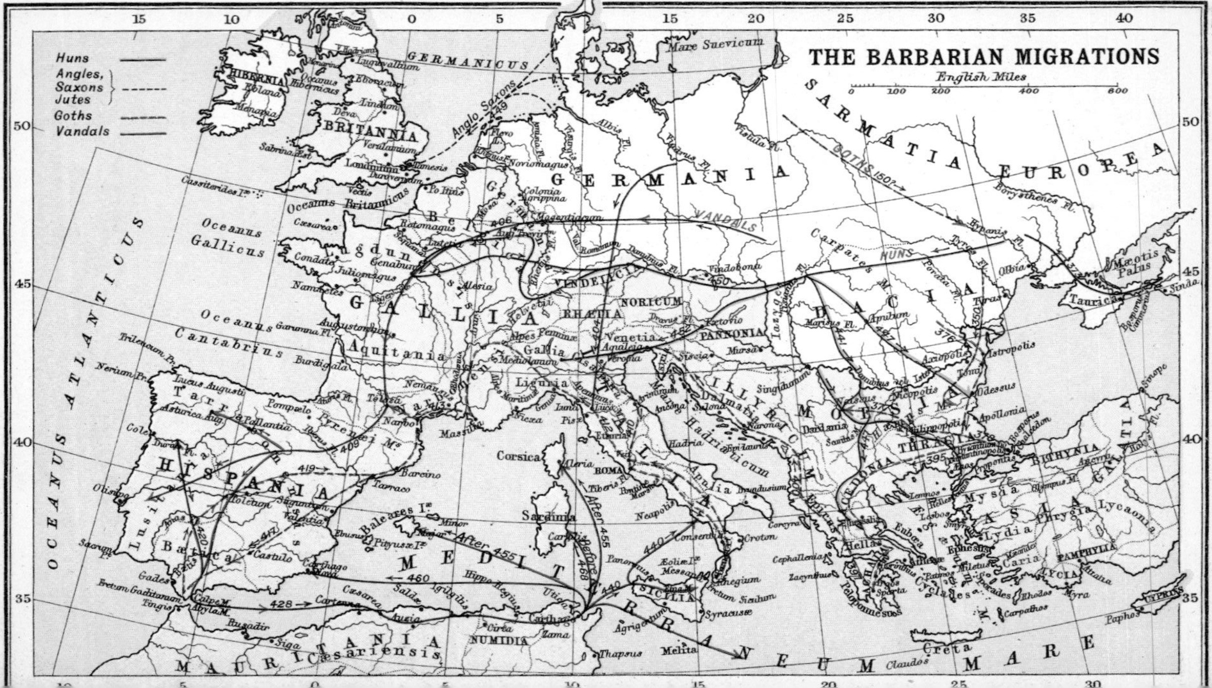

THE BARBARIAN MIGRATIONS
English Miles
0 100 200 400 600
Huns
Angles, Saxons Jutes
Goths
Vandals
GERMANICUS
SARMATIA EUROPEA
GERMANIA
GALLIA
HISPANIA
BRITANNIA
HIBERNIA
ITALIA
DACIA
MOESIA
THRACIA
MACEDONIA
ILLYRICUM
PANNONIA
NORICUM
RHAETIA
VINDELICIA
MAURITANIA Caesariensis
NUMIDIA
ASIA
BITHYNIA
GALATIA
MEDITERRANEUM MARE
OCEANUS ATLANTICUS
Oceanus Gallicus
Oceanus Cantabrius
Oceanus Britannicus
Mare Suevicum
GOTHS 150?
VANDALS
HUNS
Anglo Saxons 449
After 455
After 455
Before 468
Corsica
Sardinia
SICILIA
Creta
CYPRUS
ROMA

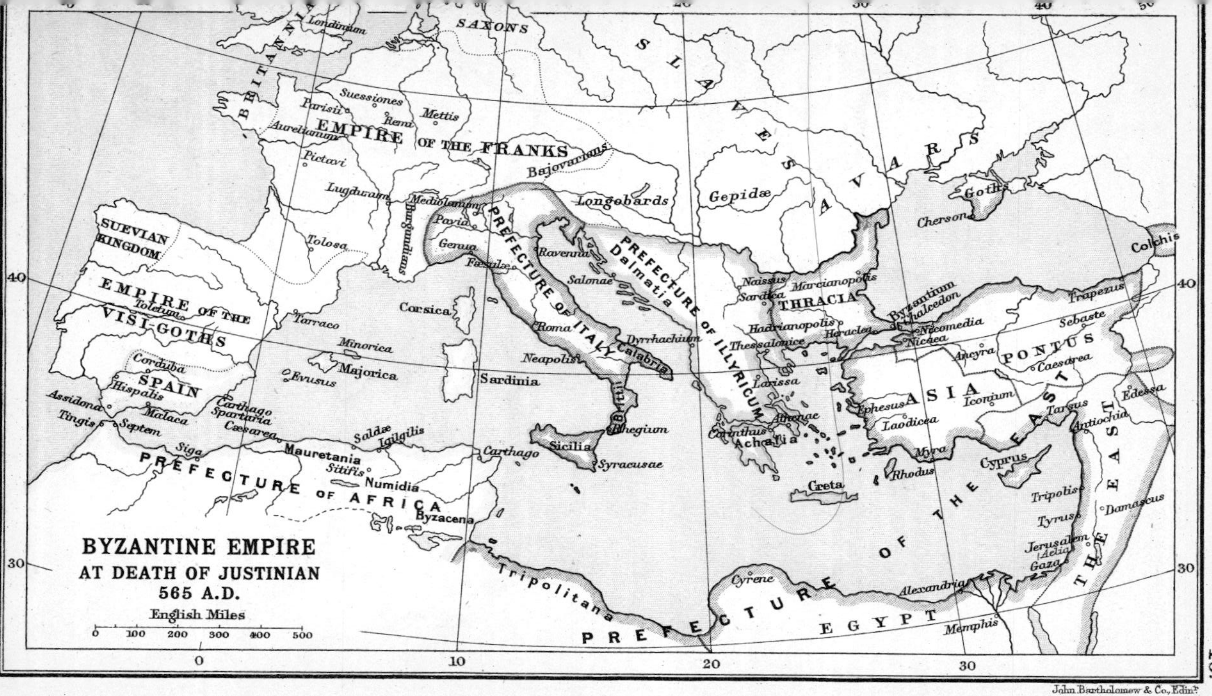
BYZANTINE EMPIRE
AT DEATH OF JUSTINIAN
565 A.D.
English Miles
0 100 200 300 400 500
SAXONS
SLAVES
AVARS
Londinium
BRITANNIA
Suessiones
Parisii
Remi
Mettis
Aurelianum
EMPIRE OF THE FRANKS
Pictavi
Bajovarians
Lugdunum
Mediolanum
Burgundians
Longobards
Gepidæ
Goths
Cherson
Colchis
SUEVIAN KINGDOM
Tolosa
Pavia
Genua
Ravenna
Fæsulæ
PREFECTURE OF ITALY
PREFECTURE OF ILLYRICUM
Dalmatia
Salonae
EMPIRE OF THE VISI-GOTHS
Toletum
Corsica
Tarraco
Roma
Minorica
Majorica
Evusus
Neapolis
Dyrrhachium
Calabria
Corduba
SPAIN
Hispalis
Sardinia
Bruttii
Rhegium
Assidona
Tingis
Septem
Malaca
Carthago Spartaria
Cæsarea
Siga
Saldæ
Igilgilis
Mauretania
Sitifis
Numidia
Carthago
Sicilia
Syracusae
PREFECTURE OF AFRICA
Byzacena
Tripolitana
Naissus
Sardica
Marcianopolis
THRACIA
Byzantium
Chalcedon
Hadrianopolis
Heraclea
Nicomedia
Nicæa
Thessalonice
Larissa
Athenae
Corinthus
Achaia
Trapezus
Sebaste
PONTUS
Caesarea
Ancyra
ASIA
Iconium
Ephesus
Laodicea
Myra
Rhodus
Creta
Cyprus
Tarsus
Antiochia
Edessa
Tripolis
Damascus
Tyrus
Jerusalem
(Aelia)
Gaza
PREFECTURE OF THE EAST
Cyrene
Alexandria
EGYPT
Memphis
40
30
0
10
20
John Bartholomew & Co., Edin.

EUROPE
AT THE
DEATH OF CHARLEMAGNE
814 A.D.
English Miles
0 50 100 200 300 400 500
NORTHMANNALAND
PICTISH KM
SCOTS KINGDOM
BRITISH KINGDOMS
ENGLISH KINGDOMS
OCCIDENTALIS
OCEANUS
Bebbanbyrig
Eoforacum
Lundenwic
DANIA
Haethum
ABODRITI
WILZI
Brema
SAXONIA
Orheim
THURINGIA
SORABI
Ganda
Landen
Aachen
Colonia
AUSTRIA
Fulda
Ratumagus
Treveris
Remi
Parisii
NEUSTRIA
Mogontia
Mettis
Reganesburg
BRITANNIA
LIMES BRITANNICUS
Aurelianum (Orleans)
Turones
Namnetes
ALSATIA
Strassburg
ALMANNIA
BAIOARI
KINGDOM OF THE FRANKS
Autun
Cabillio
RETIA
Salzburg
Poitiers
BURGUNDIA
Lugdunum
AQUITANIA
Aureliacum (Aurillac)
Genua
Burdigala
Vienna
Medtolanum
Verona
Oveum
KINGDOM OF THE ASTURIAS
GALLAECIA
WASCONIA
Papia
KINGDOM OF ITALY
Portugalim
Tolosa
Avenio (Avignon)
Arelas (Arelate)
Genua
Florentia
LIMES HISPANICUS
GOTHIA
Massilia
OMAYYAD EMIRATE OF KURTUBA
Saragocia
Olizbona
Spoleto
CORSICA
Barcinona
Tulaitala
Batalyus
Maiorica
Balensiya
Sardinia
Neapolis
BALEARICUM MARE
Kurtuba
Caralis
Kadis
Xeres
EAST
Kartagenna
Panormus
Tanga
Wahran
El-Gezair
Buna
Kartago
Susa
Kerwân
CALIPHATE

FINNISH RACES
OSTARSALT
ESTHONIA
Novgorod
MORDVINS
PETCHENEGS
KINGDOM OF THE KHAZARS
MACEDONIA OR SLAVANIA
Kiev
Nitrava
Cumeoberg
KINGDOM OF THE AVARS
ATELCUSU
Chersona
Sugdaa
BULGARIAN Km.
CROBATIA
PONTICUM MARE
Jadera
Spalatum
Naisus
Sardica
Barna
Sinope
Constantinopolis
Trapezus
SCLAVINIA
Adrianopolis
Chalcedon
Nicomedia
Barium
Dyrrhachium
Thessalonice
Ancyra
Brundisium
Caesarea
ROMAN EMPIRE
Philadelphia
Iconium
Halab (Aleppo)
Athenae
Antiochia
Patrae
Attalea
Cyprus
Tarabulus
Damascus
Tyrus
Creta
Yafa
Jerusalem
Dimyat
Barka
Alexandria
Fustat
OF THE ABBASIDS
John Bartholomew & Co., Edinr.

Shetland Is.
Orkney Is.
Hebrides
Iona
SCOTLAND
Aberdeen
St. Andrews
Glasgow
NORTH SEA
ATLANTIC OCEAN
Armagh
Tuam
IRELAND
Dublin
Cashel
Bangor
York
Chester
St. Asaph
Lincoln
Norwich
ENGLAND
St. Davids
St. Albans
London
Salisbury
Winchester
Canterbury
Chichester
NORWAY
Bergen
Hamar
Aslo
Viborg
Aarhuus
DENMARK
Ribe
Roskilde
Schleswig
Oldenburg
Hamburg
Ratzeburg
Schwerin
Bremen
Minden
Verden
Havelberg
Utrecht
Munster
Magdeburg
Paderborn
Merseburg
Naumburg
Cologne
Liège
Cambrai
Rouen
Amiens
St. Pol de Léon
Aleth
Dol
Quimper
Chartres
Paris
Rheims
Verdun
Mayence
Treves
Würzburg
Worms
Bamberg
Spires
Metz
Toul
Vannes
Nantes
Orléans
Tours
Sens
Eichstädt
Strassburg
Freising
Augsburg
Basel
Bourges
FRANCE
Poitiers
Besançon
Constance
Angoulême
Limoges
Chur
ROMAN CATHOLIC OR W
Clermont
Lyons
Geneva
Milan
Verona
Aquila
Bordeaux
le Puy
Moutiers
Vienne
Mantua
Padua
Mende
Embrun
Parma
Bologna
Auch
Albi
Avignon
Toulouse
Nîmes
Arles
Aix
Narbonne
Marseilles
Pisa
Florence
Santiago-de-Compostella
Lugo
Leon
Braga
Zamora
Burgos
Osma
Pamplona
Lamego
Salamanca
Saragossa
Huesca
Coimbra
Avila
Segovia
SPAIN
Lisbon
Toledo
Barcelona
Tarragona
Evora
Badajoz
Valencia
Silves
Balearic Isles
Palma
Seville
Granada
Cartagena
Corsica
Aleria
Ajaccio
Torres
Sardinia
Oristano
Cagliari
Perugia
Viterbo
Rome
Palermo
Carthage
Bona
MEDITE
Note
Christians at the end of 2nd Century
" from 2nd to 5th "
" " 5th " 9th "
" " 9th " 12th "
" " 12th " 14th "
Division between the Eastern & Western Churches
Mohammedanism is shown by bands of colour
Bishoprics
Archbishoprics
Archb. of the Greek Church
Patriarchates
English Miles
0 50 100 200 300 400 500

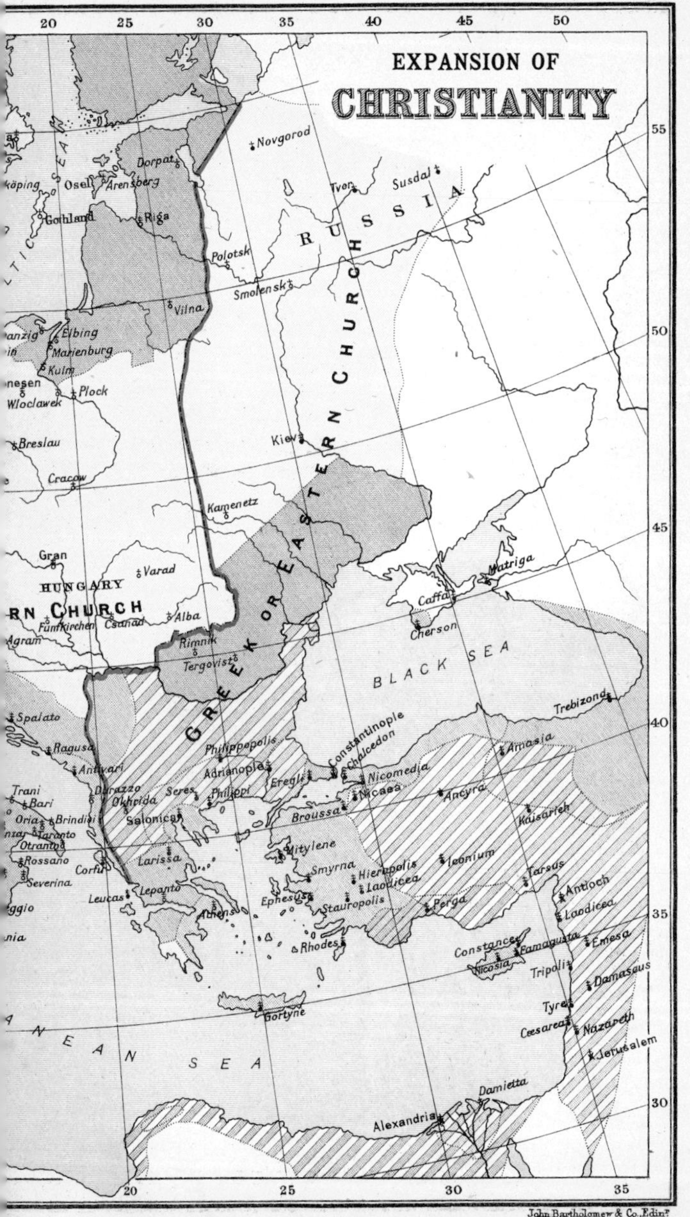

John Bartholomew & Co. Edin^r

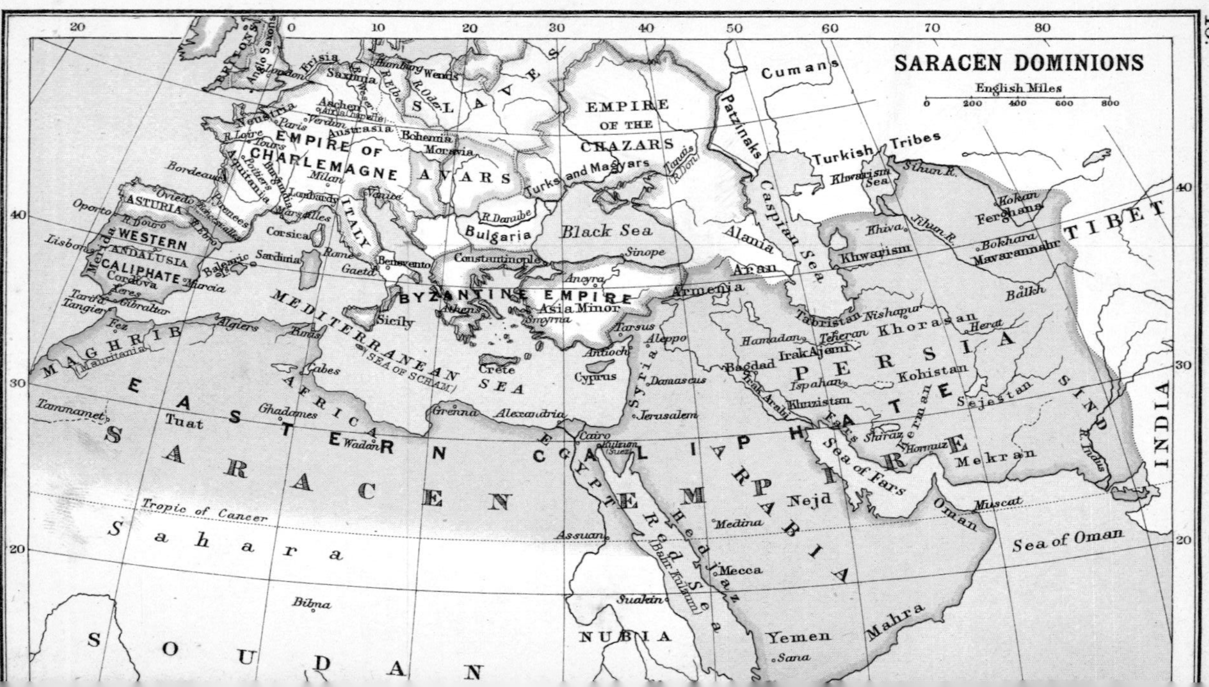
SARACEN DOMINIONS
English Miles
0 200 400 600 800
EMPIRE OF CHARLEMAGNE
EMPIRE OF THE CHAZARS
BYZANTINE EMPIRE
WESTERN CALIPHATE
EASTERN CALIPHATE
SARACEN
SLAVES
AVARS
ITALY
Bulgaria
Asia Minor
Black Sea
Caspian Sea
MEDITERRANEAN SEA
(SEA OF SCHAM)
Red Sea
(Bahr Kulzum)
Sea of Fars
Sea of Oman
Khwarism Sea
Cumans
Patzinaks
Turkish Tribes
Turks and Magyars
Alania
Aran
Armenia
Syria
PERSIA
Khorasan
Kohistan
Sejestan
Kerman
Mekran
Fars
Irak Ajemi
Irak Arabi
Khuzistan
Tabristan
Khwarism
Mavarannahr
Ferghana
Kokan
Bokhara
Balkh
Herat
Nishapur
Teheran
Hamadan
Ispahan
Shiraz
Hormuz
Bagdad
Aleppo
Damascus
Jerusalem
Antioch
Tarsus
Cyprus
Crete
Sinope
Ancyra
Smyrna
Constantinople
Athens
Sicily
Benevento
Gaeta
Rome
Venice
Lombardy
Milan
Corsica
Sardinia
Balearic Is.
Marseilles
Burgundia
Aquitania
Poitiers
Tours
Paris
Neustria
Austrasia
Verdun
Aachen
Aix la Chapelle
Saxonia
Frisia
London
Anglo Saxons
BRETONS
R. Loire
R. Weser
R. Elbe
R. Oder
R. Danube
Tanais
R. Don
Hamburg
Wends
Bohemia
Moravia
Bordeaux
Pyrenees
Roncesvalles
R. Ebro
R. Douro
ASTURIA
Oviedo
Oporto
Lisbon
Merida
ANDALUSIA
Cordova
Murcia
Xeres
Tarifa
Gibraltar
Tangier
Fez
MAGHRIB
Mauritania
Algiers
Tunis
Cabes
AFRICA
Ghadames
Wadan
Tuat
Tammamet
Grenna
Alexandria
Cairo
Kulzum
(Suez)
EGYPT
Assuan
Suakin
NUBIA
ARABIA
Hedjaz
Medina
Mecca
Nejd
Yemen
Sana
Mahra
Oman
Muscat
Sahara
Tropic of Cancer
Bilma
SOUDAN
Sihun R.
Jihun R.
Khiva
TIBET
SIND
R. Indus
INDIA

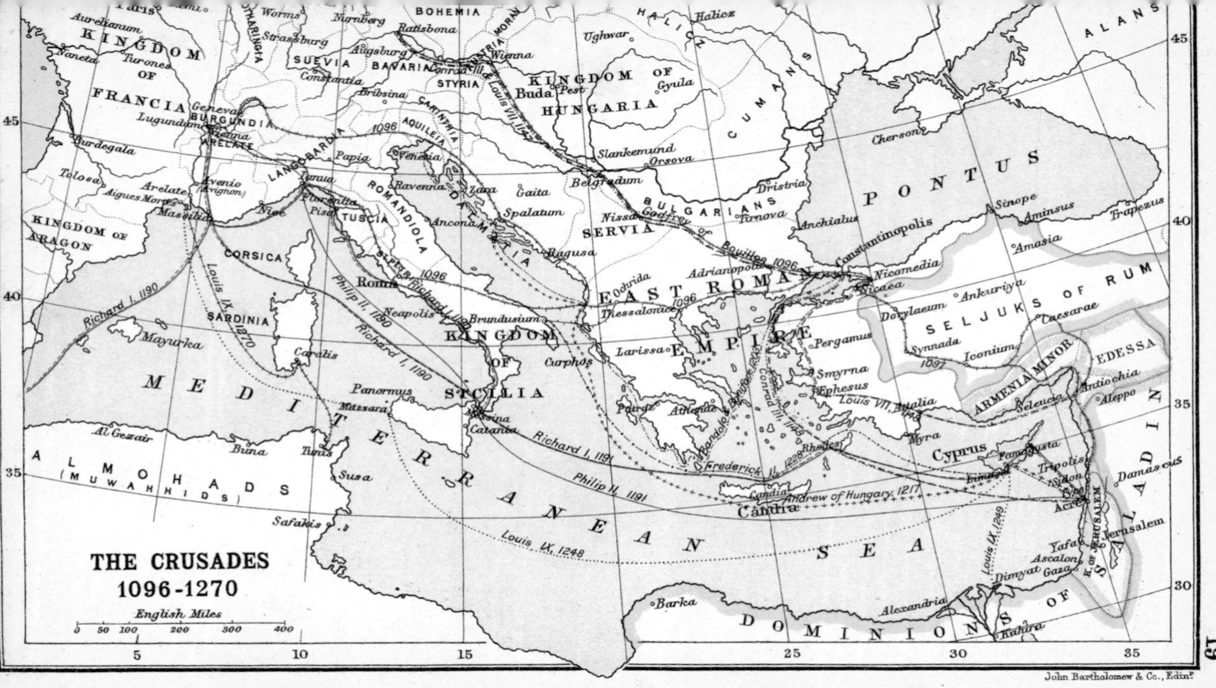
THE CRUSADES
1096-1270
English Miles
0 50 100 200 300 400
KINGDOM OF FRANCIA
BURGUNDIA
ARELATE
KINGDOM OF ARAGON
LANGOBARDIA
ROMANDIOLA
TUSCIA
DALMATIA
KINGDOM OF SICILIA
CORSICA
SARDINIA
SUEVIA
BAVARIA
BOHEMIA
STYRIA
CARINTHIA
AQUILEIA
KINGDOM OF HUNGARIA
HALICZ
CUMANS
ALANS
BULGARIANS
SERVIA
EAST ROMAN EMPIRE
PONTUS
SELJUKS OF RUM
ARMENIA MINOR
EDESSA
K. OF JERUSALEM
SALADIN'S DOMINIONS
ALMOHADS (MUWAHHIDS)
MEDITERRANEAN SEA
Cyprus
Candia
Paris
Aurelianum
Naneta
Turones
Lugundunum
Geneva
Vienna
Burdegala
Tolosa
Arelate
Aigues Mortes
Avenio (Avignon)
Massilia
Nice
Genua
Pisa
Florentia
Papia
Venetia
Ravenna
Ancona
Roma
Neapolis
Brundusium
Zara
Spalatum
Ragusa
Gaita
Worms
Strassburg
Nurnberg
Ratisbona
Augsburg
Constantia
Brixina
Wienna
Buda
Pest
Gyula
Ughwar
Halicz
Slankemund
Orsova
Belgradum
Nissa
Dristria
Tirnova
Ochrida
Adrianopolis
Thessalonica
Larissa
Athenae
Patrae
Curphos
Constantinopolis
Anchialus
Cherson
Sinope
Aminsus
Trapezus
Amasia
Nicomedia
Nicaea
Dorylaeum
Ankuriya
Caesarae
Synnada
Iconium
Pergamus
Smyrna
Ephesus
Atalia
Myra
Rhodes
Seleucia
Antiochia
Aleppo
Famagusta
Tripolis
Sidon
Tyre
Acre
Damascus
Jerusalem
Yafa
Ascalon
Gaza
Dimyat
Kahira
Alexandria
Barka
Mayurka
Caralis
Panormus
Mazzara
Messina
Catania
Al Gezair
Buna
Tunis
Susa
Safakis
Richard I. 1190
Richard I. 1191
Philip II. 1190
Philip II. 1191
Louis IX. 1248
Louis IX. 1249
Louis IX. 1270
Louis VII. 1147
Conrad III. 1147
Conrad III. 1148
Godfrey of Bouillon 1096
Frederick II. 1228
Andrew of Hungary 1217
Dandolo & Boniface 1202
1096
1097
John Bartholomew & Co., Edin.

EUROPE
AT THE
TIME OF THE CRUSADES
1189
English Miles
0 50 100 200 300 400
ATLANTIC
OCEAN
NORTH
SEA
KINGDOM
OF
NORWEGIA
Bergen
Tonsberg
SCOTIA
Abberden
Edwinesburg
HIBERNIA
Divelin
Limeric
Dunholm
Eboracum
ANGLIA
Londoniae
Bristol
Exancestre
Ripa
Sleswig
HOLSATIA
SLAVINIA
FRISIA
Brema
HOLLAND
WESTPHALIA
SAXONIA
BRABANT
Colonia
Aachen
HASSIA
BRANDENBURG
Treveri
Moguntia
LOTHARINGIA
Worms
FRANCIA
Swinfurt
Nurnberg
ROMAN EMPIRE
Strassburg
SUEVIA
Augsburg
BAVARIA
Constantia
Brixina
BURGUNDIA
Geneva
Vienna
ARELATE
LANGOBARDIA
Mediolanum
Papia
Ianua
Florentia
TUSCIA
ROMANDIOLA
Roma
Neapol
Rothomagus
Paris
Remi
Aurelianum
KINGDOM
OF
FRANCIA
Naneta
Turones
Lugundum
Burdegala
Tolosa
Arelate
Avenio
(Avignon)
Massilia
Nice
KINGDOM OF
LEON
Oveum
Portugalim
Kᴹ OF PORTUGAL
Olizbona
Kᴹ OF NAVARRE
Tudela
KINGDOM
OF
CASTILIA
Toletum
KINGDOM OF
ARAGON
Barchinona
Balensiya
Batalyus
Kurtuba
ALMOHADS
(MUWAHHIDS)
Kadis
Almeriya
Tanga
Mayurka
WEST
CORSICA
SARDINIA
Caralis
MEDITE
Panormus
Wahran
Al Gezair
Buna
Tunis
Susa
Safakis
ALMOHADS
(MUWAHHIDS)

VIATKA
KAMA
Bulgar
Braschimo
Kostroma
Susdal
Ladoga
TERRITORY OF NOVGOROD
Novgorod
Pskov
Dorpat
ESTHONIA
Sigtuna
SUECIA
VARANGIAN SEA
LITHUANIA
POLOTSK
Polotsk
Tver
Moscow
RUSSIA
MORDVINS
Ryesan
Smolensk
Minsk
Grodno
Gdansk
PRUZZIANS
YATVEGS
KINGDOM OF POLONIA
Wratislavia
Ratibor
Kursk
Tchernigov
Putivil
Pinsk
Turov
Breze
Valdimir
KIEV
Kiev
Bereyaslavl
POLOVZIANS
KHAZARS
Sarub
Sendomir
Peremyshl
HALICZ
Halicz
CUMANS OR
ALANS
MORAVIA
Wienna
Ughwar
Gran
KINGDOM OF HUNGARIA
Buda
Pest
Gyula
Matracha
Cherson
Slankemund
Sirmium
Orsova
Belgradum
Dristria
PONTUS
BULGARIANS
Tirnova
Nissa
SERVIA
Spalatum
Sardica
Ragusa
Philippopolis
Anchialus
Constantinopolis
Sinope
Aminsus
Trapezus
Amasia
Adrianopolis
Nicomedia
Nicaea
EAST ROMAN EMPIRE
Sipontum
Durazzo
Thessalonice
Larissa
Carphos
Dorylaeum
Ankuriya
SELJUKS OF RUM
Caesarae
Pergamus
Iconium
ARMENIA MINOR
Tarsus
Antiochia
Seleucia
Smyrna
Ephesus
Attalia
Myra
Patras
Athenae
Cyprus
Famagusta
Tripolis
Damascus
Candia
SEA
Yafa
Jerusalem
Dimyat
Barka
Alexandria
Kahira
DOMINIONS OF SALADIN
20
25
30
35
40
45
50
55
John Bartholomew & Co., Edinr.

NORSE-VIKING INVASIONS
KINGDOM OF CANUTE
English Miles
0 50 100 200 300
The Danelaw
Norse Settlements
Arctic Circle
Far Oer Is
Shetland Is
Orkney Is
KINGDOM OF THE ISLES
SCOTTISH KINGDOM
Lothians
STRATHCLYDE
Carham
NORTHUMBRIA
Bernicia
Deira
Man
IRELAND
NORTH WALES
MERCIA
EAST ANGLIA
Assandun
Maldon
Essex
London
Kent
Sussex
WESSEX
Penselwood
Brentford
Sherston
W. WALES
NORTH SEA
NORWAY
(Northmen)
Trondhjem
Bergen
Tunsberg
SWEDEN
Gothland
Scania
DENMARK
Slaves
Saxony
FRIESLAND
ROMAN EMPIRE
Lotharingia
Bohemia
NORMANDY
BRITTANY

ANGLO-SAXON BRITAIN
"THE HEPTARCHY."
English Miles
0 10 20 40 60 80
PICTS
Forth
Alcluyd
STRATHCLYDE
GALLOWAY
Tweed
Lindisfarne
BERNICIA
NORTHUMBRIA
Tyne
Jarrow
Durham
Tees
Whitby
Daegsastan ⚔603
Man
Swale
DEIRA
York
Wharfe
Heathfield ⚔633
Humber
Manchester
LINDSEY
Dore
Trent
Lincoln
Chester ⚔607 & 613
Faddiley ⚔584
Nottingham
Derby
Maserfield ⚔642
Stafford
NORTH STAMFORD GYRWE
MIDDLE ANGLES
Lichfield
Tamworth
Leicester
NORTH
Severn
MERCIA
(MIERCE)
SOUTH GYRWE
EAST ANGLES
Bridgenorth
Warwick
Fen
Ouse
St. Edmundsbury
WALES
HWICCE
SOUTH ANGLES
Severn
Gloucester
Burford
Witham
Hertford
EAST SAXONS
Oxford ⚔774
Ashdown ⚔871
Bensington ⚔777
MIDDLE SAXONS
London
Thames
Deorham ⚔577
Englefield ⚔871
Reading ⚔871
Chippenham
Merton ⚔871
Wedmore
WESSEX
Ethandun ⚔878
Ockley ⚔851
KENT
Athelney
Ellandun ⚔825
Winchester
Wilton ⚔871
Sherborne
SOUTH SAXONS
Wareham
Wight
Hengests Dun ⚔836
WEST WALES
FRISIA
4
2
0
56
54
52
50
John Bartholomew & Co., Edinr.

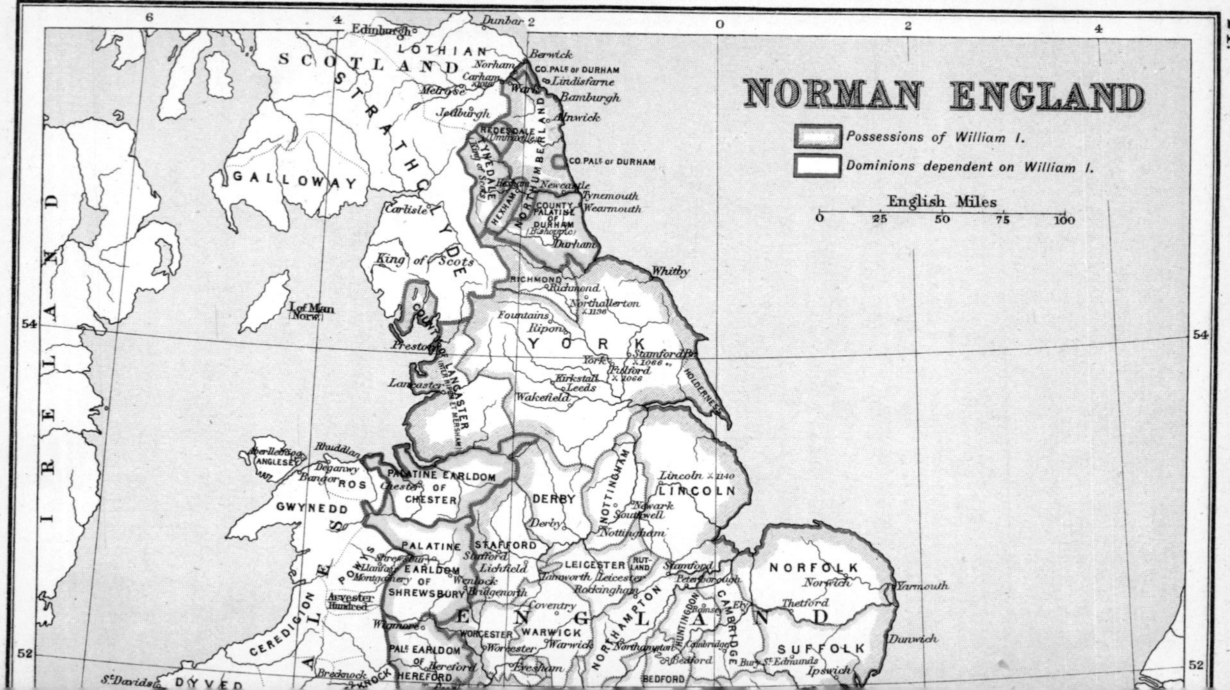
NORMAN ENGLAND
Possessions of William I.
Dominions dependent on William I.
English Miles
0
25
50
75
100
SCOTLAND
LOTHIAN
STRATHCLYDE
King of Scots
GALLOWAY
Edinburgh
Dunbar
Berwick
Norham
Carham
Melrose
Jedburgh
Carlisle
CO. PAL. OF DURHAM
Lindisfarne
Bamburgh
Alnwick
Wark
NORTHUMBERLAND
REDESDALE
TYNEDALE
(King of Scots)
HEXHAM
Newcastle
Tynemouth
Wearmouth
COUNTY PALATINE OF DURHAM
(Bishopric)
Durham
RICHMOND
Richmond
Northallerton
YORK
Whitby
Fountains
Ripon
York
Stamford Br.
Fulford
Kirkstall
Leeds
Wakefield
HOLDERNESS
COUNTY OF LANCASTER
(INTER RIPAM ET MERSHAM)
Preston
Lancaster
I. of Man
(Norw.)
LINCOLN
Lincoln
Newark
Southwell
Nottingham
NOTTINGHAM
DERBY
Derby
RUTLAND
LEICESTER
Leicester
Tamworth
Stamford
Peterborough
Rockingham
NORTHAMPTON
Northampton
HUNTINGDON
Ramsey
CAMBRIDGE
Cambridge
Ely
Bedford
BEDFORD
NORFOLK
Norwich
Thetford
Yarmouth
SUFFOLK
Bury St. Edmunds
Ipswich
Dunwich
ENGLAND
STAFFORD
Stafford
Lichfield
Coventry
WARWICK
Warwick
Evesham
WORCESTER
Worcester
Bridgenorth
Wenlock
PALATINE EARLDOM OF SHREWSBURY
Shrewsbury
Montgomery
POWYS
Arvester Hundred
PALATINE EARLDOM OF CHESTER
Chester
PAL. EARLDOM OF HEREFORD
Hereford
Wigmore
Brecknock
Rhuddlan
Deganwy
Bangor
ROS
GWYNEDD
ANGLESEY
CEREDIGION
WALES
DYVED
St. Davids
IRELAND

F R A N C E
County of Flanders
Ponthieu
Amiens
Vermandois
Beauvais
Champagne
Isle of France
Chartres
Orleannois
Perche
NORMANDY
MAINE
BRITTANY
Boulogne
Etaples
Calais
Arras
Amiens
Compiegne
Beauvais
Gisors
Paris
Mantes x 1087
Etampes
Orleans
Eu
Arques x 1053
Aumale
Mortemer x 1054
Vernon
Andelys
Rouen
Longueville
Fécamp
Harfleur
Jumieges
Evreux
Conches
Ivry
Verneuil
Montfort
Honfleur
Lisieux
Val-es-dunes x 1047
Falaise
Mortagne
Bellême
Belesme
Le Mans
Alençon
Caen
Harcourt
Tinchebrai x 1106
Domfront
Bayeux
Coutances
Granville
Mortain
Avranches
Pontorson
Fougeres
Cherbourg
Mt. St. Michel
Dol x 1076
Rennes
St. Malo
St. Helier
Jersey
Sark
Alderney
Guernsey
Channel Islands
38 m.
31 m.
St. Malo to Southampton 151 m.
to Southampton 103 m.
Rohan
Ushant I.
KENT
SUSSEX
SURREY
MIDDLESEX
HANTS
BERKS
WILTS
SOMERSET
DORSET
DEVON
CORNWALL
Sandwich
Dover
Canterbury
Hythe
Rye
Winchelsea
Hastings
Senlac 1066
Pevensey
Rochester
Tonbridge
London
Waltham
Lewes
Chichester
Arundel
Selsea
Reading
Wallingford
Waverley
Alton
Winchester
Romsey
Southampton
Alwinestune
I. of Wight
Salisbury
Wilton
Marlborough
Devizes
Malmesbury
Bath
Bristol
Wells
Glastonbury
Chepstow
Wimborne
Wareham
Poole
Dorchester
Bridport
Montacute
Ilchester
Cardiff
Llandaff
Dunster
Bampton
Exeter
Dartmouth
Trematon
Bodmin
St. Neot
St. Michael
50
48
4
2
0
John Bartholomew & Co., Edin.

NORTH SEA
IRISH SEA
ENGLISH CHANNEL
St Georges Chan.
North Chan.
Bristol Chan.
ENGLAND
IRELAND
LOTHIAN
STRATHCLYDE
GALLOWAY
Berwick District
NORTHUMBERLAND
DURHAM
CUMBERLAND
WESTMORELAND
WELSH PRINCIPALITIES
WELSH MARCHER EARLDOMS
ULTONIA (ULSTER)
CONNACTIA (CONNAUGHT)
MIDIA (MEATH)
LACENNIA (LEINSTER)
MOMONIA (MUNSTER)
HOLLAND
BRABANT
AMIENS
VERMANDOIS
LORRAINE
I. of Man (Norwegian)
Anglesea
Dublin
York
Chester
Lincoln
Norwich
Fornham
Oxford
LONDON
Canterbury
Dover
Hastings
Winchester
Salisbury
Bristol
Exeter
Calais
Boulogne
Bouvines
Amiens
Utrecht
I. of Wight
Lundie Is

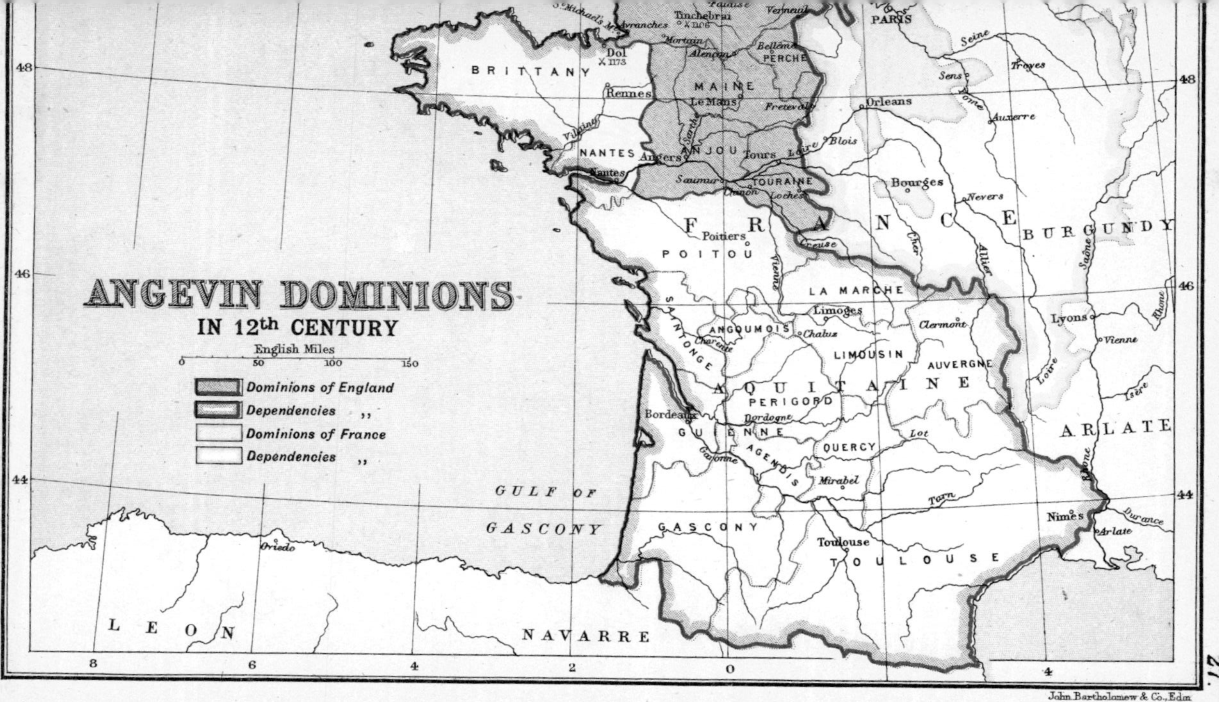
ANGEVIN DOMINIONS
IN 12th CENTURY
English Miles
0 50 100 150
Dominions of England
Dependencies ,,
Dominions of France
Dependencies ,,
BRITTANY
Dol
1173
Rennes
Vilaine
NANTES
Nantes
Angers
ANJOU
Tours
Loire
Blois
Saumur
Chinon
Loches
TOURAINE
MAINE
Le Mans
Sarthe
Fretevall
Alençon
Mortain
Avranches
Tinchebrai
1106
Verneuil
Bellême
PERCHE
PARIS
Orleans
Seine
Sens
Yonne
Auxerre
Troyes
Bourges
Nevers
Cher
Allier
FRANCE
BURGUNDY
Saône
Rhone
Lyons
Vienne
Loire
Isère
ARLATE
Durance
Arlate
Nimes
Poitiers
POITOU
Vienne
Creuse
LA MARCHE
Limoges
Chaluz
ANGOUMOIS
Charente
SAINTONGE
LIMOUSIN
Clermont
AUVERGNE
AQUITAINE
PERIGORD
Dordogne
Bordeaux
GUIENNE
Garonne
AGENOIS
QUERCY
Lot
Mirabel
Tarn
Toulouse
TOULOUSE
GASCONY
GULF OF
GASCONY
Oviedo
LEON
NAVARRE
48
46
44
8
6
4
2
0
4
John Bartholomew & Co., Edin.

OTTOMAN EMPIRE
AT FALL OF CONSTANTINOPLE
1453
English Miles
0 50 100 200 300 400
Ottoman Empire
Venetian Possessions
Genoese "
Christian States of the East
KINGDOM OF THE TATARS
Cherkesses
GEORGIA
ARMENIA
AZERBIJAN
MESOPOTAMIA
EMPIRE OF THE MAMELUKES
SYRIA
TREBIZOND
BLACK SEA
OTTOMAN TURKS
KARAMAN
CYPRUS
MEDITERRANEAN SEA
HUNGARY
MOLDAVIA
WALLACHIA
BULGARIA
SERVIA
BOSNIA
Albania
ADRIATIC SEA
VENICE
PAPAL STATES
NAPLES
Sicily
Candia
Barka
Peloponnesus
Thessaly
Rhodes (To the Knights of St. John.)
Constantinople
Adrianople
Philippopolis
Trebizond
Tana
Matriga
Caffa
Soldaia
Cherson
Derbend
Tiflis
Ardahan
Kars
Erzerum
Khoi
Van
Tabriz
Maragha
Baghdad
Mosul
Nisibin
Diarbekr
Rakka
Palu
Melitene
Aleppo
Hamah
Antioch
Damascus
Tripoli
Beyrout
Tiberias
Jaffa
Jerusalem
Damietta
Alexandria
Famagusta
Nicosia
Limasol
Sinope
Samsun
Amasia
Sivas
Kaisarieh
Angora
Koniah
Karaman
Antaliya
Amastris
Heraclea
Scutari
Ismid
Nicaea
Broussa
Gallipoli
Smyrna
Philadelphia
Ephesus
Phocaea
Chios
Samos
Lesbos
Lemnos
Euboea
Naxos
Athens
Corinth
Patras
Nauplia
Modon
Coron
Mistithra
Monembasia
Cerigo
Canea
Candia
Thessalonica
Larissa
Zeitun
Lepanto
Parga
Janina
Castoria
Ochrida
Butrinto
Corfu
Nicopolis
Cephalonia
Zante
Durazzo
Antivari
Cattaro
Ragusa
Mostar
Spalato
Zara
Kosovo
Krushevatz
Nish
Sofia
Widin
Nicopoli
Sistova
Tirnova
Silistria
Varna
Burgas
Kilia
Odessa
Jassy
Temesvar
Semlin
Belgrade
Esseg
Venice
Pola
Ravenna
Florence
Rome
Naples
Benevento
Bari
Taranto
Messina
Reggio
Catania
Malta
Benghazi
Derna
R. Danube
R. Drave
R. Save
Kazil Irmak
R. Kur
R. Aras
R. Tigris
R. Euphrates

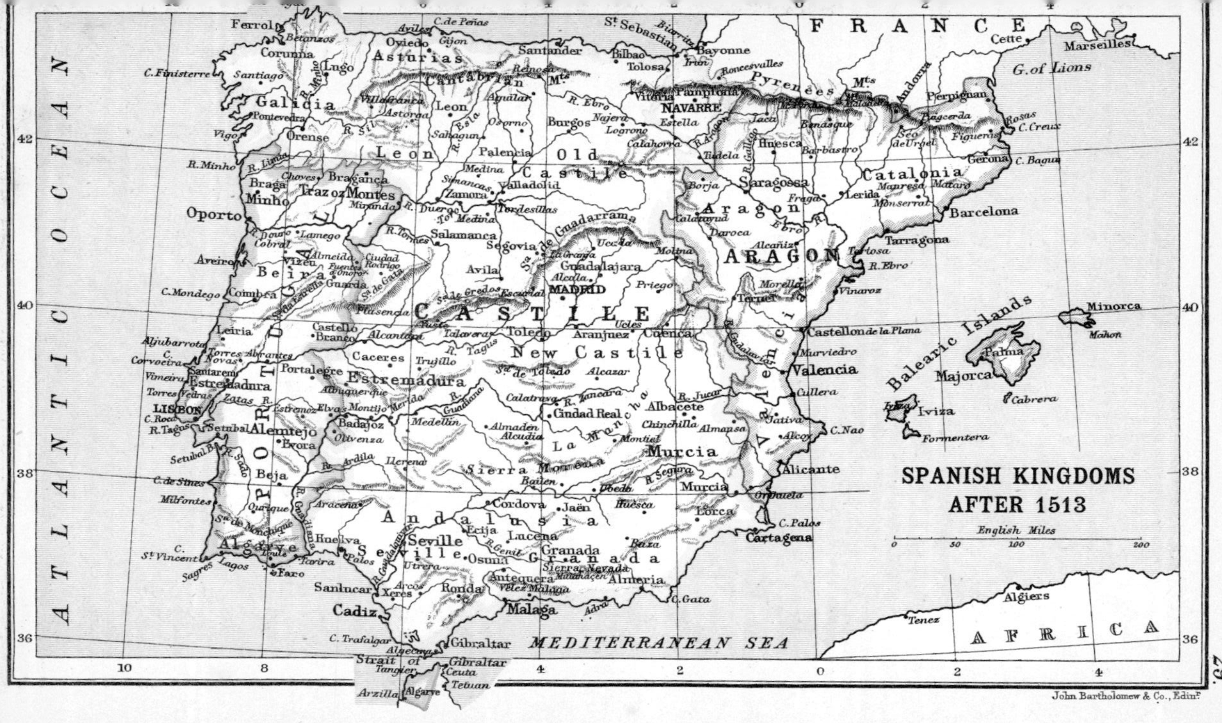
SPANISH KINGDOMS
AFTER 1513
English Miles
0
50
100
200
FRANCE
AFRICA
MEDITERRANEAN SEA
ATLANTIC OCEAN
G. of Lions
Balearic Islands
Minorca
Mahon
Majorca
Palma
Cabrera
Iviza
Formentera
NAVARRE
ARAGON
Aragon
CASTILE
Old Castile
New Castile
Catalonia
Valencia
Murcia
Granada
Andalusia
Estremadura
Leon
Asturias
Galicia
PORTUGAL
Beira
Alemtejo
Algarve
Minho
Traz oz Montes
La Mancha
MADRID
LISBON
Oporto
Barcelona
Saragossa
Toledo
Seville
Cordova
Cadiz
Malaga
Gibraltar
Cartagena
Alicante
Pyrenees Mts.
Cantabrian Mts.
Sierra Morena
Sierra Nevada
Sa. de Guadarrama
Strait of Gibraltar
Ceuta
Tangier
Tetuan
Algiers
Tenez
Bayonne
Marseilles
Perpignan
John Bartholomew & Co., Edin.r

GERMANY & N. ITALY
END OF 15th CENTURY
SCHLESWIG
HOLSTEIN
MECKLENBURG
POMERANIA
KAMMIN
BREMEN
OLDENBURG
E. FRIES LAND
FRIESLAND
UTRECHT
MÜNSTER
HOLLAND
GUELDERS
ZEELAND
BRUNSWICK LÜNEBURG
RUPPIN
BRANDENBURG
MAGDEBURG
ANHALT
LIPPE
RAVENS BERG
CLEVE
MARK
WESTPHALIA (To Cologne)
EICHS FELD
SAXONY
SILESIA
FLANDERS
BRABANT
JÜLICH
BERG
COLOGNE
HESSE
LIEGE
HAINAUT
NASSAU
HENNEBERG
TREVES
LUXEMBURG
VALOIS
PALATINATE
NAS.
MAYENCE
WÜRZBURG
NUREMBERG
UPPER PALATINATE
BOHEMIA
Schleswig
Kiel
Rendsburg
Eutin
Rügen
Stralsund
Rostock
Wismar
Güstrow
Lübeck
Mecklenburg
Ratzeburg
Hamburg
Schwerin
Waren
Stargard
Stettin
Usedom
Kammin
Friedland
Flatow
Hemmingstedt
Meldorf
Ritzbüttel
Ameland
Terschelling
Vlieland
Texel
Groningen
Leeuwarden
Stavoren
Aurich
Emden
Jever
Oldenburg
Bremen
Lauenburg
Lüneburg
Dannenberg
Verden
Perleberg
Wittstock
Lychen
Schwedt
Königsberg
Bernstein
Pyritz
Ruppin
Chorin
Havelberg
Stendal
Berlin
Cölln
Lebus
Frankfurt
Schwerin
Posen
Gnesen
Harlem
Amsterdam
Harderwijk
Zwolle
Bentheim
Deventer
Zutphen
Utrecht
Rotterdam
Meppen
Hoya
Diepholz
Celle
Hanover
Minden
Osnabrück
Tecklenburg
Schauenburg
Hildesheim
Brunswick
Wolfenbüttel
Magdeburg
Brandenburg
Storkow
Beeskow
Jüterbog
Schwiebus
Krossen
Münster
Goslar
Halberstadt
Zerbst
Wittenberg
Luckau
Kottbus
Guben
Sorau
Sagan
Glogau
Ravenstein
Cleve
Breda
Bergen
Wesel
Gueldres
Mörs
Dortmund
Soest
Paderborn
Corvey
Göttingen
Einbeck
Anhalt
Nordhausen
Halle
Leipzig
Wurzen
Bruges
Ghent
Antwerp
Mechlin
Alost
Ypres
Lille
Tournai
Arras
Mons
Maubeuge
Cambrai
Avesnes
Brussels
Maastricht
Liege
Namur
Aix-la-Chapelle
Jülich
Limburg
Cologne
Siegen
Cassel
Waldeck
Hersfeld
Marburg
Giessen
Wetzlar
Sondershausen
Merseburg
Mühlhausen
Eisenach
Erfurt
Gotha
Orlamünde
Schwarzburg
Naumburg
Gera
Altenburg
Dresden
Meissen
Chemnitz
Bautzen
Görlitz
Liegnitz
Breslau
Schweidnitz
Bischofswerda
Aussig
Leitmeritz
Glatz
Greiz
Plauen
Brüx
Kaaden
Fulda
Coburg
Hof
Blankenheim
Coblenz
Nassau
Prüm
Rense
Frankfurt
Wiesbaden
Hanau
Schweinfurt
Podiebrad
Ziskaberg
Prague
Carlsbad
Eger
Bömish Brod
Kuttenberg
Chrudim
Peronne
Guise
Marle
Noyon
Laon
Coucy
Roucy
Soissons
Rheims
Mouzon
Rethel
Grand Pré
Bouillon
Sedan
Vianden
Luxemburg
Simmern
Mayence
Sponheim
Treves
Darmstadt
Worms
Wertheim
Würzburg
Bamberg
Bayreuth
Pilsen
Mies
Taus
Deutsch-Brod
Iglau
Tabor
Brünn
Kaiserslautern
Spires
Mosbach
Zweibrücken
Heidelberg
Windsheim
Sulzbach
Rothenburg
Nuremberg
Amberg
Riesenberg
Dammartin
Verdun
Saarbrücken
Metz
Landau
Heilbronn
Hall
Weissenburg
Regensburg
Znaim
Chalons
R. Elbe
R. Oder
R. Ems
R. Spree
R. Warthe
R. Rhine
R. Meuse
R. Scheldt
R. Moselle
R. Marne
R. Moldau

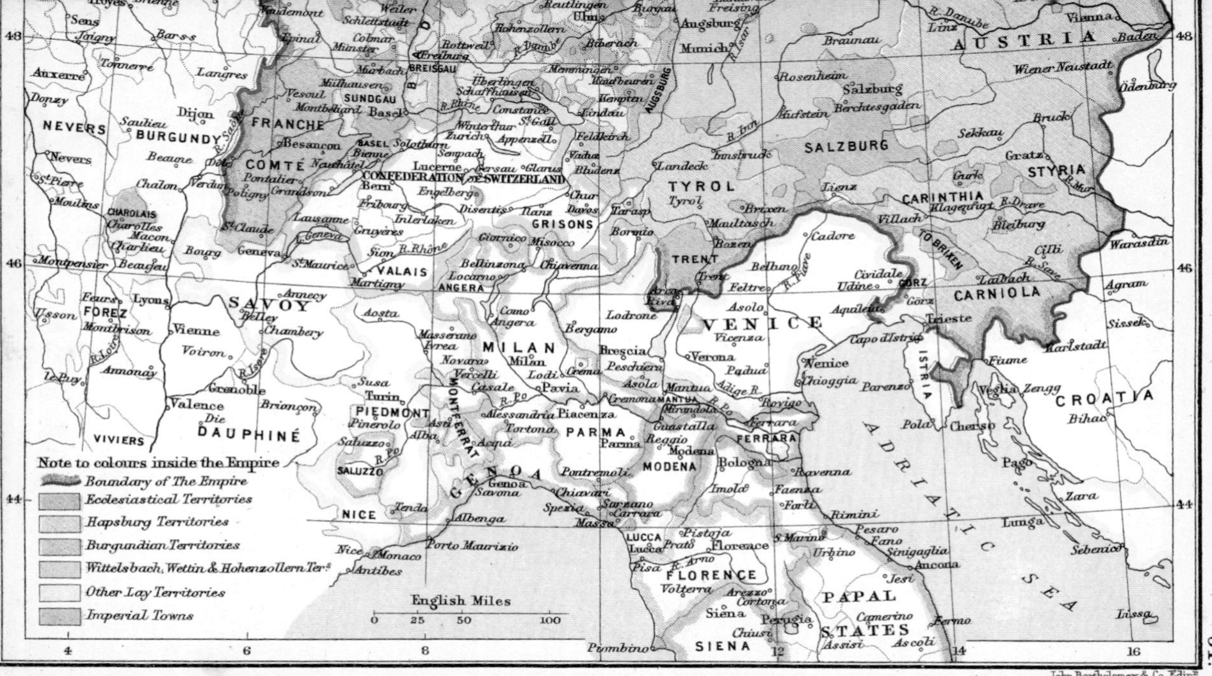
AUSTRIA
SALZBURG
STYRIA
CARINTHIA
CARNIOLA
TYROL
TRENT
TO BRIXEN
GÖRZ
VENICE
ISTRIA
CROATIA
ADRIATIC SEA
FRANCHE COMTÉ
BURGUNDY
NEVERS
CHAROLAIS
FOREZ
VIVIERS
DAUPHINÉ
SAVOY
VALAIS
CONFEDERATION of SWITZERLAND
GRISONS
SUNDGAU
BREISGAU
BASEL
AUGSBURG
ANGERA
MILAN
MONTFERRAT
PIEDMONT
SALUZZO
NICE
GENOA
PARMA
MANTUA
MODENA
FERRARA
LUCCA
FLORENCE
SIENA
PAPAL STATES
R. Danube
R. Rhône
R. Po
R. Arno
R. Inn
R. Isar
R. Saône
R. Loire
R. Isère
R. Piave
R. Adige
R. Drave
R. Save
R. Mur
Vienna
Munich
Augsburg
Salzburg
Innsbruck
Trent
Venice
Milan
Turin
Genoa
Florence
Geneva
Lyons
Dijon
Bern
Basel
Note to colours inside the Empire
Boundary of The Empire
Ecclesiastical Territories
Hapsburg Territories
Burgundian Territories
Wittelsbach, Wettin & Hohenzollern Ters.
Other Lay Territories
Imperial Towns
English Miles
0 25 50 100
John Bartholomew & Co., Edinr.

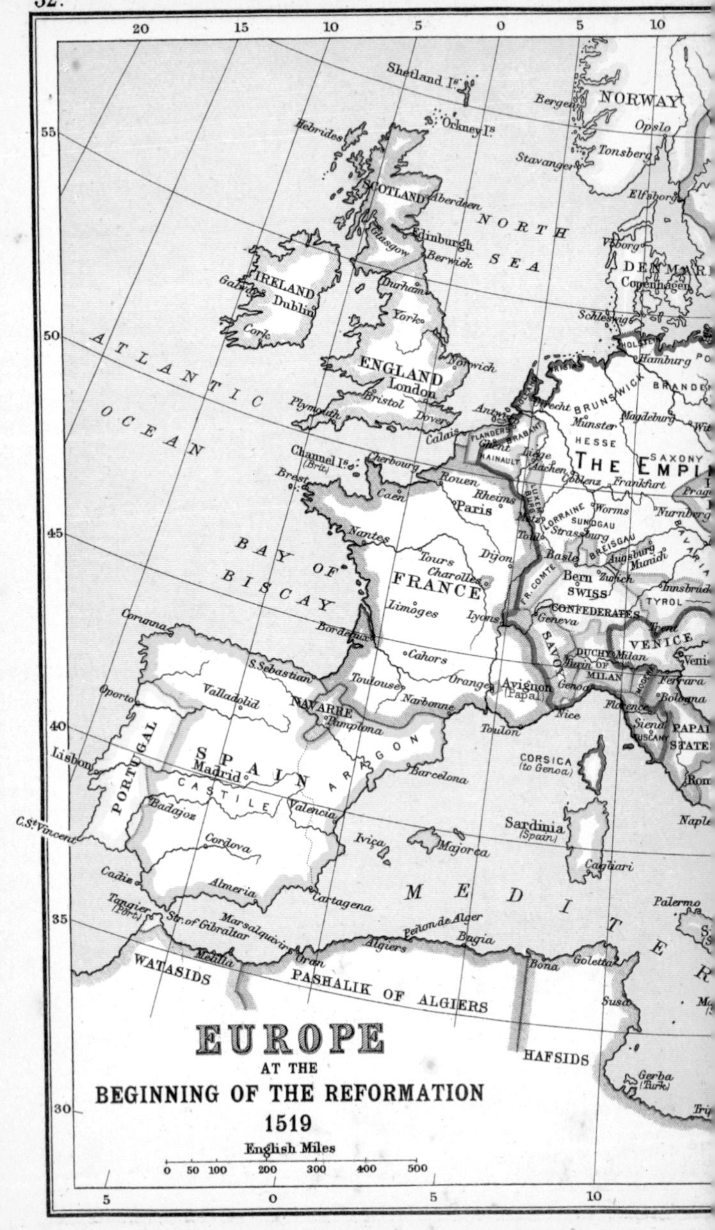
EUROPE
AT THE
BEGINNING OF THE REFORMATION
1519
English Miles
Shetland Is.
Orkney Is.
Hebrides
NORWAY
Bergen
Opslo
Stavanger
Tonsberg
Elfsborg
SCOTLAND
Aberdeen
Edinburgh
Glasgow
Berwick
NORTH SEA
IRELAND
Galway
Dublin
Cork
Durham
York
ENGLAND
London
Norwich
Bristol
Plymouth
Dover
Calais
ATLANTIC OCEAN
DENMARK
Copenhagen
Schleswig
Hamburg
BRUNSWICK
Magdeburg
Münster
HESSE
SAXONY
THE EMPIRE
Antwerp
Utrecht
FLANDERS
BRABANT
Ghent
HAINAULT
Liège
Aachen
Coblenz
Frankfurt
Channel Is. (Brit.)
Cherbourg
Brest
Caen
Rouen
Rheims
Paris
LORRAINE
Worms
Nurnberg
Metz
Toul
Strassburg
SUNDGAU
BREISGAU
Augsburg
Munich
BAVARIA
Nantes
BAY OF BISCAY
Tours
Dijon
Charolles
FRANCE
Basle
Zurich
Bern
SWISS CONFEDERATES
FR. COMTE
Innsbruck
TYROL
Limoges
Lyons
Geneva
Trent
VENICE
Corunna
Bordeaux
Cahors
SAVOY
DUCHY OF MILAN
Milan
Turin
S. Sebastian
Toulouse
Orange
Avignon (Papal)
Genoa
Ferrara
Bologna
Oporto
Valladolid
NAVARRE
Pamplona
Narbonne
Florence
Siena
TUSCANY
PAPAL STATES
Toulon
Nice
Lisbon
PORTUGAL
SPAIN
Madrid
CASTILE
ARAGON
Barcelona
CORSICA (to Genoa)
Badajoz
Valencia
C. St. Vincent
Sardinia (Spain)
Iviça
Majorca
Cordova
Cagliari
Cadiz
Almeria
Cartagena
MEDITERRANEAN
Palermo
Tangier (Port.)
Str. of Gibraltar
Marsalquivir
Peñon de Alger
Bagia
Melilla
Oran
Algiers
Bona
Goletta
WATASIDS
PASHALIK OF ALGIERS
Susa
HAFSIDS
Gerba (Turk)

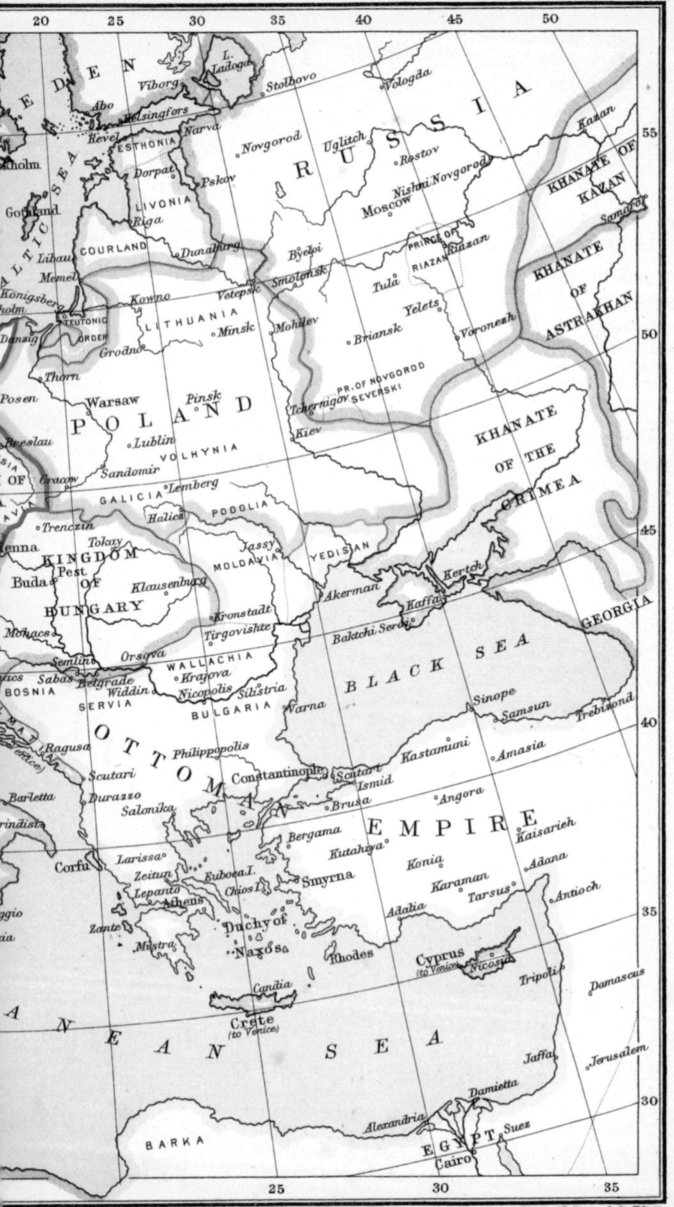

John Bartholomew & Co., Edin.

ENGLAND
WALES
ENGLISH CHANNEL
UNITED NETHERLANDS
STATES GENERAL
SPANISH NETHERLANDS
LIEGE
LUXEMBURG
CLEVE
MÜNSTER
MARK
BERG
COLOGNE
JÜLICH
GUELDERS
TREVES
PALATINATE
NASSAU
LORRAINE
METZ
SUNDGAU
CHAMPAGNE
ILE DE FRANCE
NORMANDY
MAINE
BRITTANY
ORLEANS
Channel Is.
Guernsey
Jersey
I. of Wight
Derby
Shrewsbury
Leicester
Norwich
Montgomery
Birmingham
Warwick
Naseby
Huntingdon
Newmarket
Cardigan
Worcester
Hereford
Northampton
Edge Hill
Cambridge
Carmarthen
Brecon
Gloucester
Oxford
Chalgrove
Rye House
London
Cardiff
Bristol
Bath
Newbury
Windsor
R. Thames
Sedgemoor
Canterbury
Southampton
Brighton
Hastings
Exeter
Plymouth
Falmouth
Dover
Dunkirk
Haarlem
Zaandam
Amsterdam
The Hague
Utrecht
Arnhem
Rotterdam
Dordrecht
Nymegen
Coevorden
Zwolle
Deventer
Bentheim
Steinfurt
Münster
Isselburg
Rheda
Vechta
Haselünne
Lingen
Osnabrück
Tecklenburg
RAVENSBERG
Wesel
Rheinberg
Unna
Soest
Dortmund
Mors
Breda
Ravenstein
Venlo
Flushing
Antwerp
Roermonde
Bilstein
Ostende
Bruges
Ghent
Mechlin
Hasselt
Jülich
Cologne
Siegen
Aix la Chapelle
Düren
Homburg
R. Rhine
Courtrai
R. Scheldt
Brussels
Louvain
Maastricht
Dillenburg
St. Omer
Lille
Liege
Limburg
Neuwied
Tournai
Seneffe
Fleurus
R. Meuse
Aremberg
Stavelot
Coblenz
Boulogne
St. Pol
Bethune
Mons
Namur
Prüm
Montreuil
Valenciennes
Maubeuge
Dinant
Hesdin
Arras
Cambrai
Landrecies
Avein
Lorch
Abbeville
le Câtelet
Bingen
le Tréport
Peronne
Rocroi
Bouillon
R. Moselle
Berncastel
Meisenheim
Dieppe
Amiens
Guise
Mézières
Treves
Worms
Doncherry
Sedan
Luxemburg
Birkenfeld
Fécamp
Noyon
Laon
Rethel
Ivoy
Jametz
Cherbourg
Havre
Rouen
Stenay
Thionville
Zweibrücken
Honfleur
Beauvais
Soissons
Dun
Saarbrücken
Landau
Gisors
Rheims
Grand Pré
Weissenburg
Bayeux
Elbeuf
R. Seine
Crepy
Carentan
Caen
Evreux
Châlons
Verdun
Metz
Hagenau
Coutances
Mantes
R. Marne
Clermont
Marsal
Zabern
Vire
Falaise
St. Germain
Paris
Coulommiers
Bar-le-Duc
Nancy
Strassburg
St. Pol de Léon
Versailles
Toul
Avranches
St. Malo
St. Dizier
Wittenweier
Morlaix
Provins
Brest
St. Brieuc
Lamballe
Mayenne
Mortagne
Chartres
Melun
Joinville
Vandémont
Schlettstadt
Colmar
Fontainebleau
Troyes
Sens
Chaumont
Epinal
Münster
Remiremont
Rennes
Rohan
Laval
Chateaudun
Bars-s
Wattweiler
Quimper
Châtillon
Langres
Mülhausen
Belfort
Orléans
Montargis
Joigny
Lorient
Vannes
Chât. Gontier
Vendome
Sully
Auxerre
Tonneire
Vesoul
Basel
Montbéliard
Porrentruy
la Fleche
Blois
Aubigny
Semur
Gray
Mirebeau
ANJOU
6
4
2
0
2
4
6
8
52
50
48

FRANCE
1618-1648
English Miles
0 25 50 100 150
F R A N C E
S P A I N
POITOU
AUNIS
SAINTONGE
ANGOUMOIS
MARCHE
LIMOUSIN
BOURBONNAIS
CHAROLAIS
LYONNAIS
AUVERGNE
GUIENNE AND GASCONY
LANGUEDOC
BEARN
FOIX
ANDORRA
ROUSSILLON
DAUPHINÉ
VENAISSIN
PROVENCE
SAVOY
SWITZERLAND
PIEDMONT
ASTURIAS
BASQUE PROVS
NAVARRE
LEON
OLD CASTILE
ARAGON
CATALONIA
Thouars
Châtellerault
Poitiers
Chateauroux
Sables
Luçon
Niort
I. de Ré
La Rochelle
Civray
Guéret
Montluçon
Moulins
Chalon
Charolles
Mâcon
R. Saône
R. Loire
R. Vienne
Oléron
Brouage
Rochefort
Saintes
Mortemart
Evaux
Montpensier
Roanne
Bourg
Trévoux
Angoulême
Limoges
Riom
Clermont
R. Allier
Lyons
Belley
Montbrison
Ambert
Issoire
Perigueux
Tulle
Brioude
St. Flour
Annonay
Le Puy
Vienne
Montmellian
Grenoble
Romans
Valence
R. Rhône
R. Isère
Eronsac
Bordeaux
Turenne
Sarlat
Aurillac
Duras
Biron
Cahors
R. Garonne
R. Lot
Rodez
Marvejols
Mende
Viviers
Die
Aiguillon
Agen
Albret
R. Tarn
Montauban
Alais
Orange
Uzès
Nîmes
Orignon
Moyons
Sisteron
Avignon
Forcalquier
Condom
Auch
Albi
Vabres
Lodève
Arles
Dax
Aire
Orthez
Lavour
Castres
Toulouse
Montpellier
Béziers
Cette
St. Pons
Narbonne
Carcassonne
Rieux
Pamiers
Mirepoix
Alet
Foix
Marseilles
Toulon
Aix
Brignoles
Hyères
Fréjus
Pau
Tarbes
Mauleon
Oloron
St. Bertrand
Bayonne
St. Jean de Luz
Hendaye
St. Jean Pied de Port
Santander
S. Sebastian
Bilbao
Vitoria
Pamplona
Aguilar
Frias
Haro
Burgos
Logroño
R. Ebro
Calahorra
Palencia
Jaca
Huesca
Luna
Saragossa
R. Douro
Urgel
R. Segre
Lerida
Montlouis
Bellegarde
Perpignan
Collioure
Gerona
Pontarlier
Poligny
St. Amour
Gex
Geneva
Lausanne
Sion
Martigny
Bonneville
Annecy
Aosta
Chambéry
Moutiers
St. Jean de Maurienne
Susa
Turin
Fenestrelles
Briançon
Pinerolo
Château Dauphiné
Embrun
Gap
Barcelonnette
R. Durance
Digne
Entrevaux
Vence
Grasse
Monaco
Nice
46
44
42
4
2
0
2
4
6
John Bartholomew & Co., Edinr.

GERMANY & N. ITALY
REFORMATION TO 30 YEARS WAR
1615-1648
SCHLESWIG
HOLSTEIN
MECKLENBURG
HITHER POMERANIA
FURTHER POMERANIA
BRANDENBURG
BREMEN
OLDENBURG
E. FRIES LAND
LÜNEBURG
MAGDEBURG
WOLFENBÜTTEL
LIPPE
RAVENSBERG
MÜNSTER
MARK
BERG
CLEVE
GUELDERS
JÜLICH
COLOGNE
LIEGE
SAXONY
SILESIA
BOHEMIA
MORAVIA
HESSE-CASSEL
HESSE-DARMSTADT
WALDECK
NASSAU
TREVES
LUXEMBURG
PALATINATE
UPPER PALATINATE
WÜRZBURG
ANSBACH
UNITED NETHERLANDS
STATES GENERAL
SPANISH NETHERLANDS
R. Elbe
R. Oder
R. Wartha
R. Spree
R. Eger
R. Moldau
R. Rhine
R. Meuse
R. Moselle

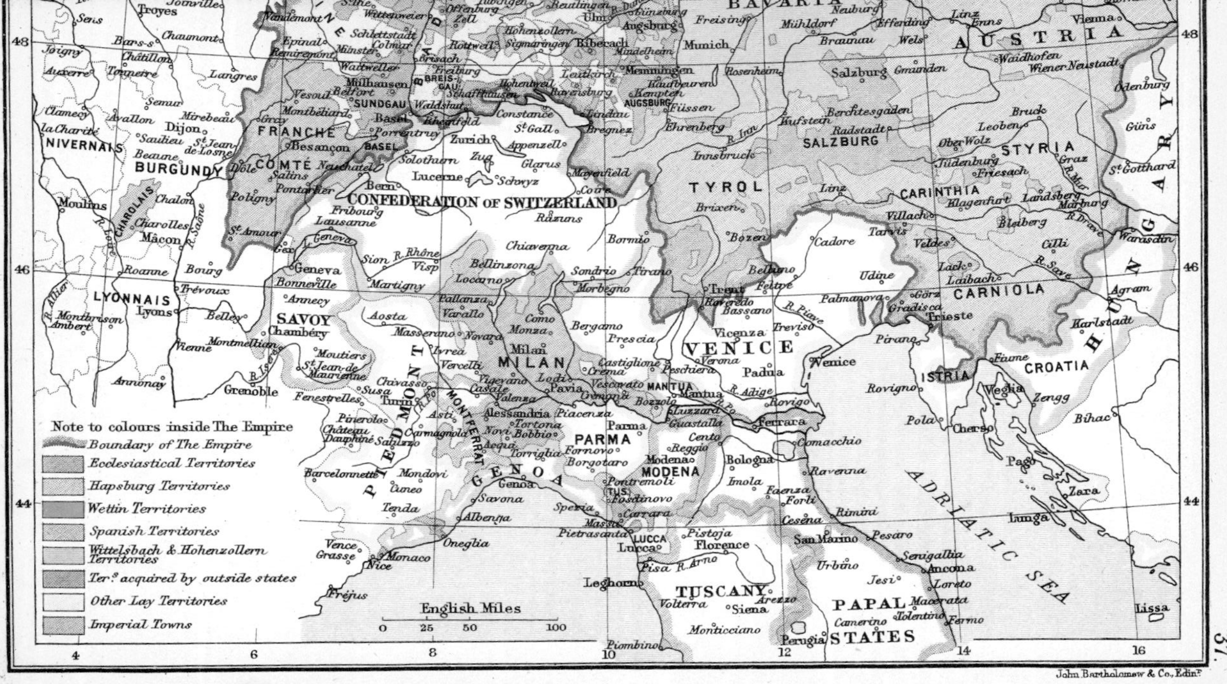

John Bartholomew & Co., Edin.r

SWITZERLAND
SAVOY
PIEDMONT
MONTFERRAT
SALUZZO
MILAN
GENOA
PARMA
MODENA
MANTUA
VENICE
LUCCA
TUSCANY
PAPAL STATES
STATO DEGLI PRESIDII
CORSICA
HUNGARY
OTTOMAN EMPIRE
Istria
Dalmatia
ADRIATIC SEA
To Venice
Sion
Domo d'Ossola
Locarno
Bellinzona
Bozen
Cadore
Trent
Belluno
Feltre
Cividale
Udine
Campoformio
Laibach
Görz
Trieste
Aosta
Masserano
Ivrea
Orta
Arona
Como
Monza
Milan
Lecco
Bergamo
Lodrone
Brescia
Chiari
Peschiera
Castiglione
Rivoli
Verona
Bassano
Asolo
Castelfranco
Treviso
Vicenza
Padua
Marano
Capo d'Istria
Venice
Vercelli
Chivasso
Susa
Fenestrelle
Turin
Casale
Vigevano
Pavia
Lodi
Crema
Cremona
Arcole
Legnago
Carpi
Monselice
Pinerolo
Carmagnola
Staffarda
Saluzzo
Cuneo
Asti
Alba
Acqui
Mondovi
Millesimo
Alessandria
Montebello
Piacenza
Bozzolo
Mantua
Luzzara
Guastalla
Polesella
Rovigo
Ferrara
Comacchio
Novi
Bobbio
S. Donino
Parma
Mirandola
Reggio
Modena
Sassuolo
Formono
Borgotaro
Torriglia
Genoa
Savona
Pontremoli
Fivizzano
Fosdinovo
Carrara
Massa
Argenta
Bologna
Casalecchio
Imola
Faenza
Modigliana
Ravenna
Cesena
Rimini
Boglio
Tenda
Loano
Albenga
Oneglia
Ventimiglia
Monaco
Nice
Spezia
Pietrasanta
Lucca
Pistoja
Prato
Florence
Pisa
R. Arno
Leghorn
Cascina
Incisa
Bibbiena
Poggibonsi
Arezzo
Volterra
Siena
Montictana
S. Marino
Urbino
Pesaro
Fano
Sinigaglia
Ancona
Jesi
Cagli
Loreto
Fabriano
R. Tiber
Fermo
Centuri
St. Florent
Calvi
Bastia
Corte
Ajaccio
Bastelica
Portovechio
Piombino
Pto. Ferrajo
Elba
Longone
Pianosa
Monte Cristo
Giglio
Talamone
Orbetello
Scarlino
S. Fiora
Orvieto
Bolsena
Castro
Viterbo
Civitavecchia
Ronciglione
Tivoli
Rome
Ostia
Velletri
Paliano
Frosinone
Sora
Foligno
Todi
Spoleto
Terni
Narni
Rieti
Amatrice
Ascoli
Civitella
Teramo
Atri
Aquila
Pescara
Ortona
Chieti
Celano
Solmona
R. Sangro
Cast. di Sangro
Larino
Termoli
S. Severo
Vieste
Mte. S. Angelo
Manfredonia
Rovigno
Albona
Cittonuova
Pola
Cherso
Veglia
Zengg
Pago
Lunga
Zara
Knin
Spalato
Brazza
Lesina
Lissa
Curzola
Lagosta
Meleda
Ragusa
Mostar
Sarajevo
Banjaluka
Karlstadt
Agram
Warasdin
R. Save
R. Drave
Fünfkirchen
Esseg
Brod
10
12
14
16
18
46
44
42

ITALY
16th TO 18th CENT.

English Miles

0 20 40 60 80 100

SARDINIA
Cast Arragonese
Terranova
Sassari
Tempio
Alghero
Posada
R. Tirso
Bosa
Macomer
Orosei
Oristano
Monte Reale
Villasor
Iglesias
Cagliari

TYRRHENIAN SEA
Ponza
Mondragone
Capua
Naples
Ischia
Castellammare
Sorrento
Capri
Nola
Avellino
Salerno
Benevento
Oliveto
Melfi
Venosa
Acerenza
NAPLES
Ruvo
Gravina
R. Bradano
Conversano
Gioia
Mola
Polignano
Monopoli
Mottola
Brindisi
Oria
Lecce
Nardo
Otranto
Castro
Gallipoli
Taranto
Potenza
Buccino
Stigliano
Capaccio
Diano
Tursi
Policastro
Francavilla
Scalea
Belvedere
Rossano
Acri
Cero
Paola
Cosenza
Amantea
Cotrone
Martorano
Policastro
Catanzaro
Squillace
Stromboli
Lipari Islands
Lipari
Ustica
Mileto
Castelvetere
Gioia
Roccella
Sciglio
Geraci
Messina
Reggio
Milazzo

MEDITERRANEAN SEA
SICILY
Trapani
Palermo
Cefalu
Naso
Patti
Castellamare
Termini
Marsala
Partanna
Corleone
Gangi
Troina
Taormina
Mazzara
Bivona
Castrogiovanne
Caltanisetta
Catania
Naro
Lentini
Girgenti
Caltagirone
Agosta
Butera
Syracuse
Alicata
Noto
Modica
Pantelleria
Biserta
Bona
Gozzo
Malta
Valetta

40 38 8 10 12 14 16 18

John Bartholomew & Co., Edinr.

CENTRAL EUROPE
1789
English Miles
0 50 100 200
Shetland Is
Orkney Is
Bergen
Christiansand
SCOTLAND
Culloden
Aberdeen
Perth
Dundee
Falkirk
Edinburgh
Glasgow
Prestonpans
NORTH SEA
Belfast
Drogheda
IRELAND
Galway
Dublin
Cork
Carlisle
Newcastle
York
Preston
Liverpool
Chester
Wales
ENGLAND
Birmingham
Cardiff
Bristol
London
Sedgemoor
Dover
Land's End
Tönning
Amsterdam
Utrecht
UNITED NETHERLANDS
Antwerp
Brussels
AUSTRIAN NETHERLANDS
Liege
Cologne
Münster
ATLANTIC
OCEAN
English Channel
Cherbourg
Havre
Caen
Brest
Rennes
Paris
Versailles
Chartres
R. Seine
Rheims
Verdun
Metz
Toul
Mayence
Fontainebleau
Orleans
Strassburg
Angers
R. Loire
Dijon
Mulhausen
Montbeliard
Nantes
Tours
Nevers
Besançon
Basel
Neuchatel
Bern
SWITZER
FRANCE
Bay of
Biscay
Montpensier
Pompadour
Lyons
Geneva
Savoy
PIEDMONT
(To Sardinia)
Bordeaux
Grenoble
R. Rhone
Valence
Turin
Agen
R. Garonne
Orange
Avignon
Bayonne
Toulouse
Pau
Narbonne
Marseilles
Nice
Toulon
Andorra
Coruña
C. Finisterre
Pontevedra
Oviedo
Leon
Pamplona
Burgos
R. Ebro
Braga
Oporto
R. Douro
Saragossa
Cardona
Gerona
Coimbra
Ciudad Rodrigo
Lerida
Corsica
Ajaccio
SPAIN
Madrid
Tortosa
Barcelona
PORTUGAL
Lisbon
R. Tagus
Alcantara
Toledo
R. Guadiana
Minorca (Brit.)
Port Mahon
SARDINIA
Badajoz
Olivenza
Valencia
Palma
Majorca
laCarolina
Iviza
Cordova
Murcia
Alicante
Sagres
Lagos
Seville
Granada
Cartagena
MEDITE
Cadiz
Malaga
Gibraltar (Br.)
Algiers
la Calle
Bona
Tangier
Ceuta (Span.)
Melilla (Span.)
Oran (Span.)
FEZ & MOROCCO
ALGIERS
10
0
50
40

John Bartholomew & Co., Edinr.

CENTRAL EUROPE
1810
English Miles
0 100 200
Shetland Is.
Orkney Is.
Bergen
Stavenger
SCOTLAND
Aberdeen
Perth
Dundee
Edinburgh
Glasgow
Berwick
NORTH SEA
Belfast
Newcastle
Carlisle
IRELAND
Galway
Dublin
Limerick
Cork
York
Hull
Manchester
Liverpool
Wales
ENGLAND
Birmingham
Cardiff
London
Bristol
Portsmouth
Plymouth
Lands End
Dover
Heligoland (Br.)
Holland
Camperdown
The Hague
Amsterdam
Antwerp
Brussels
Lille
Ligny
Tournay
Jemappes
Cologne
Aix la Chapelle
Liege
Berg
Nassau
Boulogne
ATLANTIC OCEAN
English Channel
Cherbourg
Channel Is. (Br.)
Havre
Amiens
Rouen
Laon
Craonne
Luxemburg
Mayence
Vauchamps
Valmy
Kaiserslautern
Paris
Montmirail
Metz
Fere
Arcis
Fontainebleau
Montereau
La Rothiere
Bar
Strassburg
Baden
Brest
Rennes
Vannes
Le Mans
Orleans
R. Loire
Tours
Dijon
Nantes
FRANCE
Basel
Valençay
Nevers
Neuchâtel
Bern
La Rochelle
Rochefort
Bay of Biscay
Limoges
R. Saône
Geneva
Lyons
Chambery
Perigueux
Clermont
Bordeaux
Grenoble
Turin
R. Garonne
R. Rhône
Valence
Novi
Savona
C. Finisterre
Coruña
Lugo
S. Sebastian
Santander
Espinosa
Bayonne
Orthes
Nimes
Avignon
Toulouse
Nice
Cannes
Burgos
Vitoria
Marseilles
Toulon
Carvalho
Medino de Rio Seco
R. Ebro
Andorra
Oporto
Tudela
Lerida
Gerona
Corsica
Ajaccio
R. Douro
Almeida
Salamanca
Saragossa
Busaco
Coimbra
Ildefonso
Belchite
PORTUGAL
Ciudad Rodrigo
SPAIN
Barcelona
Tarragona
Tortosa
Madrid
Vimeira
Torres Vedras
Cintra
Lisbon
R. Tagus
Talavera
Almonacid
Ocaña
Ucles
Badajoz
R. Guadiana
Murviedro
Valencia
Balearic Isles
Minorca
Majorca
Iviza
SARDINIA
Albuera
Medellin
Ciudad Real
Castalla
Cordova
Bailen
Alicante
MED
C. S. Vincent
R. Guadalquavir
Murcia
Seville
Lorca
Granada
Cartagena
Cadiz
Barossa
Malaga
C. Trafalgar
Gibraltar (Br.)
Algiers
Bona
Tangier
Ceuta
Alboran (Sp.)
Constantine
Alhucemas I.
Melilla (Sp.)
Oran
ALGIERS
Penon de Velez (Sp.)
Tlemcen
MOROCCO
10
0
50
40

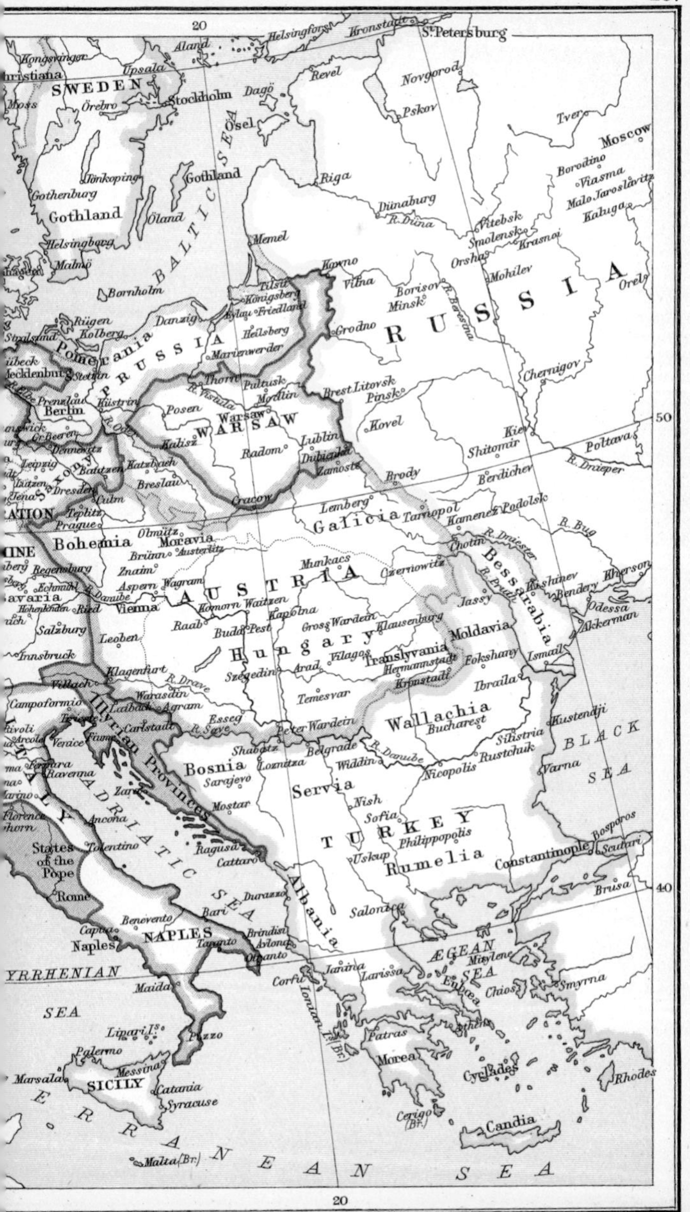

John Bartholomew & Co., Edin.r

EUROPE
1815
English Miles
0 50 100 200 300 400 500
ATLANTIC OCEAN
NORTH SEA
English Channel
Bay of Biscay
MEDITERR
IRELAND
SCOTLAND
ENGLAND
FRANCE
SPAIN
PORTUGAL
NETHERLANDS
PRUSSIA
GERMAN CONFEDER
BAVARIA
WURTEMBERG
BADEN
SAXO
SWITZERLAND
LOMBARDY-VENETIA
SARDINIA
PARMA
MODENA
TUSCANY
PAPAL STATES
DENMARK
NORWAY
KINGDOM SWEDEN AND N
MOROCCO
ALGIERS
TUNIS

Lake Ladoga
Olonetz
Viborg
Kronstadt
Helsingfors
Aland
Gefle
St. Petersburg
Vologda
G. of Finland
Reval
Stockholm
Osel
Gothland
Oland
BALTIC SEA
Pskov
Yaroslav
Kazan
R. Oka
Nijni Novgorod
Tver
Moscow
Simbirsk
Syzran
Riga
R. Duna
Vitebsk
Kaluga
Penza
R. Volga
Memel
Smolensk
RUSSIA
Saratov
Königsberg
R. Niemen
Vilna
Minsk
Orel
Danzig
W. Prussia
E. Prussia
Posen
R. Vistula
Warsaw
Chernigov
Kalisz
POLAND
R. Don
Breslau
Lublin
Kiev
Kharkov
Cracow
Berdichev
R. Dnieper
Novocherkask
Lemberg
Taganrog
Rostov
R. Dniester
Pressburg
Czernowitz
R. Pruth
Jassy
SEA OF AZOV
Kerch
Odessa
Kherson
AUSTRIA
Buda Pest
Klausenburg
Moldavia
Crimea
R. Drave
Kronstadt
Galatz
Temesvar
R. Save
BLACK SEA
Poti
Wallachia
Bucharest
Belgrade
Servia
R. Danube
Rustchuk
Varna
Sinope
Trebizond
Zara
Sarajevo
Sofia
TURKEY
Monte-negro
Cetigne
Philippopolis
Adrianople
Constantinople
Scutari
Angora
TURKEY IN ASIA
Kaisarieh
Bari
Brindisi
Salonica
Corfu
Larissa
ÆGEAN SEA
Eubœa
Konieh
Smyrna
Adana
Antioch
Ionian Is. (Br.)
Athens
Patras
Cyclades
Rhodes
Cyprus
C. Matapan
Cerigo (Br.)
Candia
Beyrout
Damascus
Jaffa
Jerusalem
SEA
Damietta
Barka
Alexandria
EGYPT
Cairo
John Bartholomew & Co., Edinr.

ARCTI
Jan Mayen
ICELAND
Reikiavik
Arctic Circle
Lofoden Is.
Malstrom
Bodö
Faroe Is.
ATLANTIC OCEAN
Shetland Is.
Rockall
BRITISH ISLES
Hebrides
C. Wrath
SCOTLAND
Aberdeen
Edinburgh
NORTH SEA
Newcastle
IRELAND
Dublin
Galway
Cork
C. Clear
Liverpool
Manchester
St. Georges Chan.
ENGLAND
Birmingham
London
Bristol
Lands End
Scilly I.
English Channel
Str. of Dover
Trondhjem
Christiansund
C. Stadt
Sogne Fd.
Bergen
Hardanger Fd.
Stavanger
Christiania
The Naze
Skager Rack
Cattegat
DENMARK
Copenhagen
Bornholm
Rügen
Göttenburg
Calmar
Heligoland
Texel
Amsterdam
Rotterdam
HOLLAND
BELGIUM
Brussels
Lille
Hamburg
Bremen
Hanover
Berlin
Prussia
GERMANY
Stettin
Dantzic
Posen
Magdeburg
Leipzig
Dresden
Cologne
Frankfort
Bohemia
Prague
Moravia
Brest
Cherbourg
Rouen
Paris
Nantes
R. Loire
Orleans
Strasburg
Bay of Biscay
FRANCE
Rochefort
Bordeaux
Lyons
Geneva
Berne
SWITZERLAND
Munich
Vienna
AUSTRI
Stuttgart
C. Ortegal
Corunna
C. Finisterre
Oporto
Coimbra
Lisbon
C. Roca
PORTUGAL
SPAIN
Madrid
Saragossa
Valladolid
Toledo
Valencia
Barcelona
Pyrenees Mts.
Toulouse
Marseilles
G. of Lions
Milan
Venice
Turin
Genoa
Trieste
Bologna
Florence
ITALY
Rome
Naples
Adriatic Sea
Bosnia
Corsica
Sardinia
Tyrrhenian Sea
Palermo
Sicily
Messina
C. Passaro
Malta
Gozo
C. St. Vincent
Cadiz
Seville
Cordova
Granada
Murcia
Malaga
Gibraltar
Str. of Gibraltar
C. Trafalgar
Cartagena
C. Gata
C. Nao
Balearic Is.
Majorca
Ivica
MEDITERRANEAN
Oran
Algiers
Tunis
C. Bon
Fez
MOROCCO
Morocco
Atlas Mts.
ALGERIA
TUNIS
G. of Cabes
Tripoli
AFRICA
Gulf of Sidra

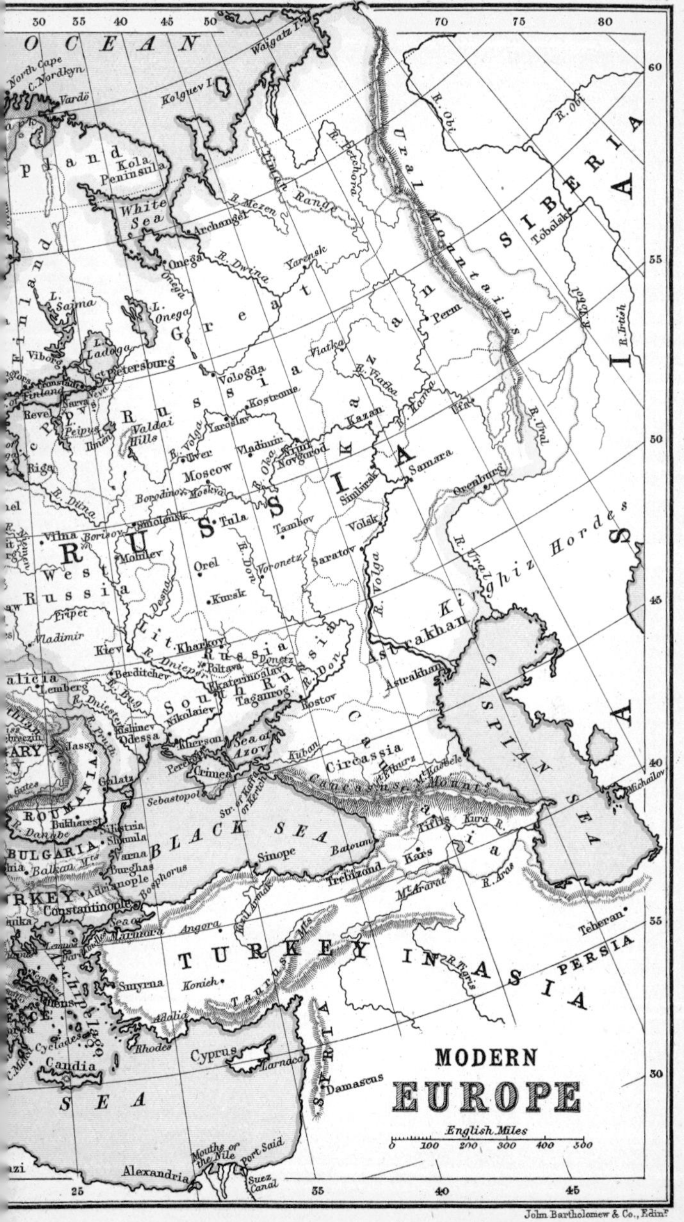
MODERN
EUROPE
English Miles
0 100 200 300 400 500
RUSSIA
Great Russia
SIBERIA
ASIA
CASPIAN SEA
BLACK SEA
TURKEY IN ASIA
PERSIA
Ural Mountains
Caucasus Mounts
Moscow
St Petersburg
Kazan
Astrakhan
Tobolsk
Archangel
Kiev
Odessa
Constantinople
Smyrna
Cyprus
Candia
Damascus
Alexandria
Port Said
Suez Canal
Teheran
John Bartholomew & Co., Edin.

Chief Industrial Districts
Coalfields
Letters indicate the nature of the Chief Industries
C Cotton I Iron L Linen M Machinery S Silk W Wool
Agriculture and Stock-rearing
Fishing
Only Navigable Rivers are shown
Principal Railways
ECONOMIC MAP OF
EUROPE
English Miles
0 100 200 300 400 500
SCOTLAND
IRELAND
ENGLAND
WALES
NORTH SEA
DENMARK
HOLLAND
BELGIUM
GERMANY
FRANCE
SWITZERLAND
SPAIN
PORTUGAL
ITALY
TUNIS
Bay of Biscay
English Channel
MEDITER.
Shetland Is.
Orkney Is.
Hebrides
Rockall
Trondhjem
Molde
Bergen
Stavanger
Christiansand
CHRISTIANIA
The Naze
The Skaw
Aberdeen
Dundee
Perth
Edinburgh
Glasgow
Wick
Londonderry
Belfast
Galway
Dublin
Limerick
Cork
Valencia I.
C. Clear
Carlisle
Newcastle
Manchester
Liverpool
Hull
Birmingham
Bristol
LONDON
Plymouth
Southampton
Dover
Lands End
Str. of Dover
Irish Sea
Heligoland
AMSTERDAM
Rotterdam
Antwerp
Calais
BRUSSELS
Luxemburg
Bremen
Hanover
Hamburg
Kiel
COPENHAGEN
Cassel
Cologne
Leipzig
Frankfurt
Metz
Strassburg
Stuttgart
Nuremberg
Munich
Basle
BERN
Innsbruck
Havre
Rouen
PARIS
Brest
Orleans
Tours
Nantes
Nevers
Dijon
Lyon
St. Etienne
Geneva
Bordeaux
Bayonne
Toulouse
Cette
Marseille
Toulon
Nice
Milan
Turin
Verona
Venice
Genoa
Florence
Leghorn
Ancona
ROME
Naples
Elba
Corsica
Ajaccio
Str. of Bonifacio
Sardinia
Sassari
Cagliari
Palermo
Sicily
Malta (British)
Tunis
Algiers
C. Ortegal
C. Finisterre
Coruña
Vigo
Oporto
Oviedo
Santander
S. Sebastian
Valladolid
Saragossa
Barcelona
LISBON
MADRID
Toledo
Valencia
Cordova
Seville
Granada
Murcia
Cartagena
Cadiz
Malaga
Gibraltar (British)
Tarifa Pt.
Balearic Is.
Majorca
Minorca
Palma
Iviza
R. Douro
R. Duero
R. Tagus
R. Ebro
Guadalquivir
R. Garonne
R. Loire
Seine
R. Rhône
Rhine
R. Elbe
R. Po
WINE
Klar R.
Channel Is.

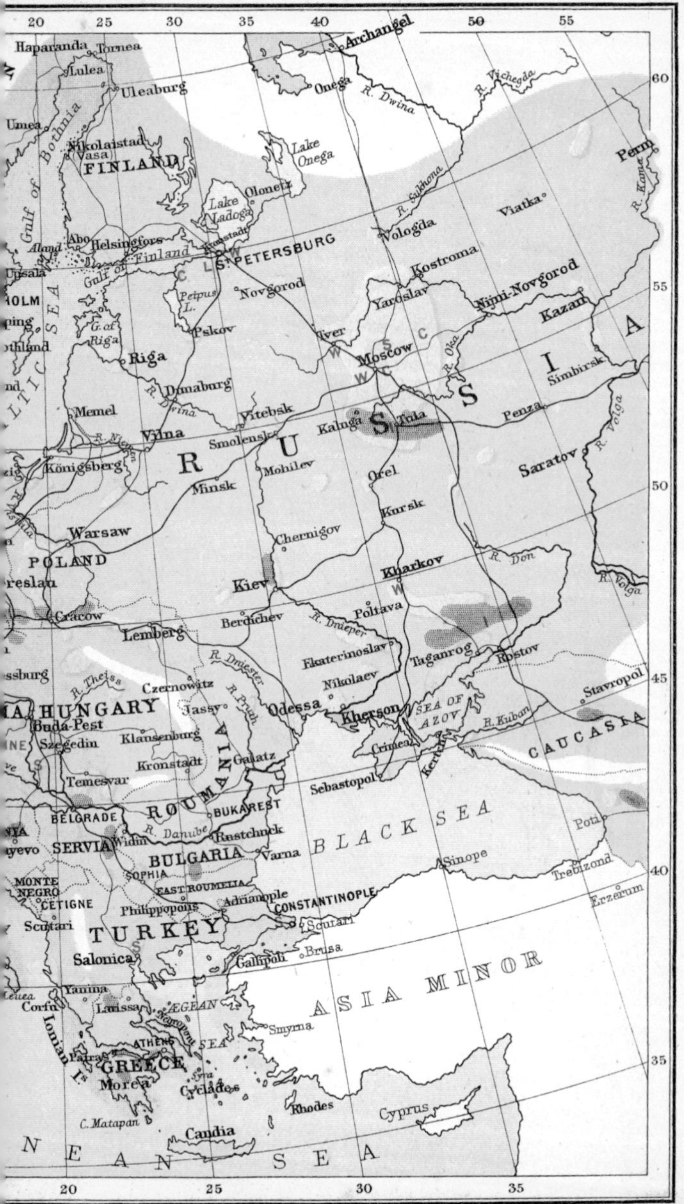
RUSSIA
FINLAND
POLAND
HUNGARY
ROUMANIA
SERVIA
BULGARIA
EAST ROUMELIA
MONTE NEGRO
TURKEY
GREECE
ASIA MINOR
CAUCASIA
BLACK SEA
SEA OF AZOV
ÆGEAN SEA
ST PETERSBURG
Moscow
Archangel
Kiev
Warsaw
Odessa
Kharkov
CONSTANTINOPLE
BUKAREST
BELGRADE
ATHENS
Buda-Pest
Riga
Vilna
Kazan
Saratov
Nijni-Novgorod
Sebastopol
Kherson
Taganrog
Rostov
Smyrna
Cyprus
Rhodes
Candia
John Bartholomew & Co., Edinr.

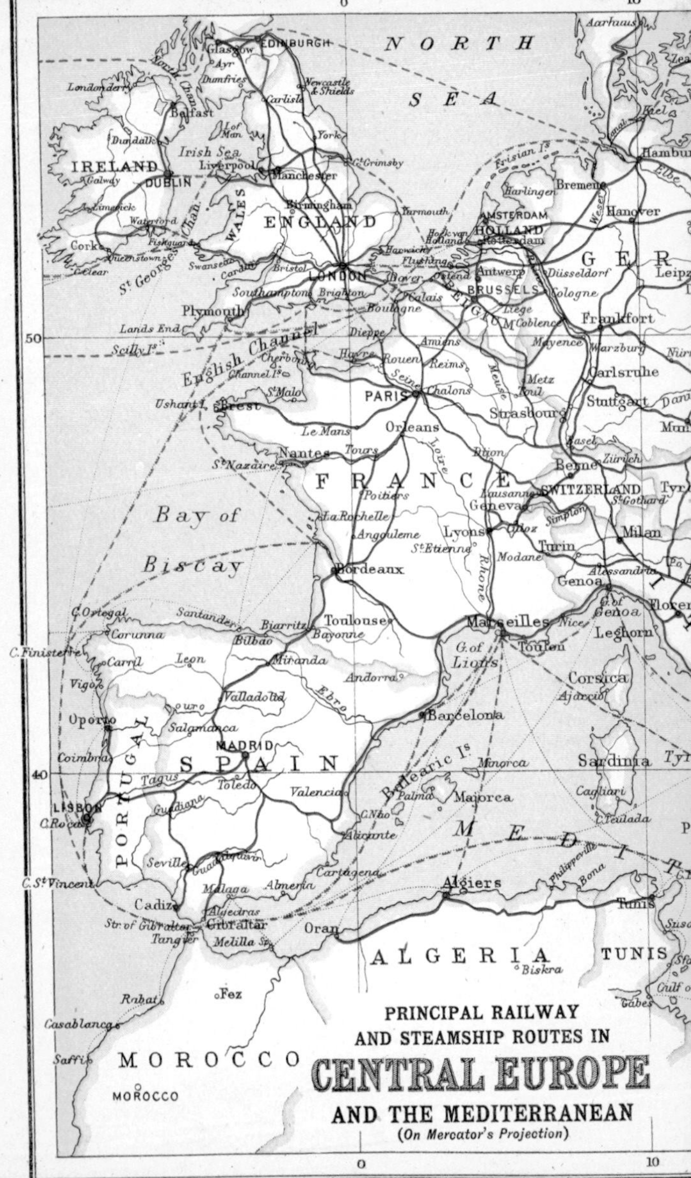
PRINCIPAL RAILWAY
AND STEAMSHIP ROUTES IN
CENTRAL EUROPE
AND THE MEDITERRANEAN
(On Mercator's Projection)
NORTH SEA
Irish Sea
English Channel
Bay of Biscay
IRELAND
ENGLAND
WALES
FRANCE
SPAIN
PORTUGAL
SWITZERLAND
HOLLAND
ALGERIA
TUNIS
MOROCCO
Corsica
Sardinia
Balearic Is
Majorca
Minorca
LONDON
PARIS
MADRID
LISBON
BRUSSELS
AMSTERDAM
EDINBURGH
DUBLIN
Glasgow
Belfast
Liverpool
Manchester
Birmingham
Bristol
Plymouth
Southampton
Brighton
Dover
Calais
Boulogne
Dieppe
Havre
Rouen
Amiens
Reims
Chalons
Orleans
Le Mans
Nantes
Tours
Poitiers
La Rochelle
Angouleme
Bordeaux
Toulouse
Lyons
St Etienne
Marseilles
Toulon
Nice
Dijon
Geneva
Berne
Strasbourg
Metz
Frankfort
Cologne
Antwerp
Ostend
Flushing
Rotterdam
Hamburg
Bremen
Hanover
Milan
Turin
Genoa
Leghorn
Barcelona
Valencia
Alicante
Cartagena
Almeria
Malaga
Seville
Cadiz
Gibraltar
Tangier
Oran
Algiers
Tunis
Fez
Rabat
Casablanca
Oporto
Coimbra
Valladolid
Salamanca
Toledo
Bilbao
Santander
Biarritz
Bayonne
Corunna
Vigo
0
10
50
40

John Bartholomew & Co., Edin.

AGRICULTURAL DISTRICTS

John Bartholomew & Co., Edinr

SCOTLAND
EDINBURGH
GLASGOW
Lanark
Arran
FIRTH OF CLYDE
Ayr
Ailsa Craig
Moffat
Dumfries
Selkirk
Hawick
Jedburgh
Melrose
Kelso
R. Tweed
Cheviot Hills
NORTHUMBERLAND
Stranraer
Port Patrick
Wigtown
Whithorn
Mull of Galloway
Burrow Hd.
SOLWAY FIRTH
Carlisle
Silloth
Wigton
Maryport
Cockermouth
Workington
Whitehaven
St. Bees Hd.
CUMBERLAND
Keswick
Penrith
Appleby
WESTMORLAND
Kendal
Ravenglass
Bootle
Furness
Ulverston
Barrow in Furness
Walney I.
Dalton
R. Duddon
Morecambe Bay
Heysham
Lancaster
ISLE OF MAN
Ayre Pt.
Ramsey
Snaefell
Laxey
Douglas
Peel
Port Erin
Castletown
Calf of Man
IRISH SEA
Fleetwood
Poulton
Blackpool
St. Annes
Lytham
LANCASHIRE
Preston
Blackburn
Southport
Ormskirk
Wigan
Bolton
Bury
Rochdale
Oldham
Salford
MANCHESTER
Stockport
Formby & Hd.
New Brighton
Birkenhead
LIVERPOOL
Bootle
Warrington
Runcorn
Altrincham
Knutsford
Northwich
Macclesfield
CHESHIRE
Chester
Crewe
Nantwich
Skerries
Amlwch
Linas Hd.
Holyhead
Holy I.
ANGLESEY
Beaumaris
Aberffraw
Menai Strait
Bangor
Carnarvon
Carnarvon Bay
Snowdon
CARNARVON
Llandudno
Conway
Gt. Ormes Hd.
Beaumaris B.
Denbigh
DENBIGH
FLINT
Flint
Mold
Holywell
Ruthin
Wrexham
Ruabon
Llangollen
Nevin
Pwllheli
Port Madoc
Criccieth
Tremadoc Bay
Harlech
Bardsey I.
Braich-y-Pwll
MERIONETH
Dolgelly
Bala
Barmouth
R. Mawddach
Cader Idris
CARDIGAN BAY
Towyn
Aberdovey
R. Dovey
Aberystwith
MONTGOMERY
Montgomery
Machynlleth
Newtown
Welshpool
Llanidloes
Plinlimmon
SHROPSHIRE
Shrewsbury
Wellington
Oswestry
Ellesmere
Bridgnorth
Ludlow
Bishops Castle
Clun
Knighton
STAFFORD
Stafford
Hanley
Wolverhampton
Dudley
Kidderminster
Bewdley
5
4
3
2
55
54
53

John Bartholomew & Co. Edinr.

5 4 3 2

CARDIGAN BAY
R. Mawddach
Cader Idris
Towyn
Aberdovey
R. Dovey
Aberystwith
Aberaeron
MONTGOMERY
Montgomery
Machynlleth
Plinlimmon
Llanidloes
Newtown
Welshpool
Llanfair
SHROPSHIRE
Shrewsbury
Wellington
The Wrekin
Broseley
Much Wenlock
Church Stretton
Bishops Castle
Clun
Bridgnorth
Cleobury Mortimer
Ludlow
Knighton
Bewdley
Stourport
Kidderminster
Stourbridge
Bromsgrove
Redditch
Droitwich
Wolverhampton
Bilston
Dudley
Walsall
Penkridge
Lichfield
Rugeley
Rhayader
RADNOR
New Radnor
Presteigne
Kington
Pembridge
Weobly
Leominster
Tenbury
Bromyard
WORCESTER
Worcester
Pershore
Gt. Malvern
Ledbury
HEREFORD
Hereford
Pontrilas
Ross
Newent
Tewkesbury
Cheltenham
Gloucester
Mitcheldean
GLOUCESTER
Stroud
Cirencester
Nailsworth
Dursley
Berkeley
Wickwar
Tetbury
Malmesbury
Wootton Bassett
Chippenham
Calne
Devizes
CARDIGAN
Tregaron
Lampeter
Cardigan
Newcastle Emlyn
R. Teifi
Llandovery
Llangadock
Llandilofawr
Strumble Hd.
52
St. Davids Hd.
St. Davids
Ramsey I.
Fishguard
Newport
Presely Top
PEMBROKE
Haverfordwest
St. Brides B.
Skomer I.
Milford
Milford Haven
Narberth
Pembroke
Tenby
St. Gowans Hd.
Caldy I.
Carmarthen Bay
CARMARTHEN
Carmarthen
R. Towy
Kidwelly
Llanelly
Burry Inlet
Loughor
Swansea
Gower
Worms Hd.
Oystermouth
Mumbles
Swansea Bay
BRECKNOCK
Builth
Talgarth
Brecon
Brecknock Beacons
Crickhowell
Usk
Merthyr Tydfil
Abergavenny
Monmouth
Tredegar
Dowlais
MONMOUTH
Pontypool
Usk
Tintern Abbey
Chepstow
Risca
Caerleon
Newport
GLAMORGAN
Aberdare
Neath
Aberavon
Pontypridd
Port Talbot
Llantrissant
Kenfig
Pyle
Porthcawl
Bridgend
Caerphilly
Llandaff
Cowbridge
Penarth
Cardiff
Barry
Aberthaw
Nash Pt.
Portishead
Severn Tunnel
Avonmouth
BRISTOL
Clevedon
Yatton
Bath
Bradford
Weston super Mare
Axbridge
Cheddar
Mendip Hills
Wells
Trowbridge
Radstock
Westbury
Frome
Shepton Mallet
Warminster
Heytesbury
WILTSHIRE
Salisbury
Plain
Wylye
Wilton
Hindon
BRISTOL CHANNEL
Lundy I.
Ilfracombe
Lynton
The Foreland
Bridgewater Bay
Minehead
Exmoor Forest
Dunster
Dunkerry Beacon
Watchet
Bridgewater
Burnham
Glastonbury
Barnstaple Bay
Barnstaple
Hartland Pt.
Westward Ho
Bideford
Clovelly
S. Molton
Dulverton
SOMERSET
Quantock Hills
Taunton
Wellington
Ilchester
Yeovil
Bruton
Wincanton
Shaftesbury
51
Torrington
Chulmleigh
Tiverton
Bampton
Ilminster
Crewkerne
Chard
Sherborne
Stalbridge
Sturminster Newton
Cranborne
Bude
Bude Bay
Stratton
Hatherleigh
Holsworthy
Bow
Crediton
Cullompton
Honiton
Beaminster
Blandford
R. Stour
Wimborne
Okehampton
DEVON
Cawsand Beacon
Exeter
Axminster
Axmouth
Lyme Regis
Bridport
DORSET
Bere Regis
Poole
Tintagel Cas.
Camelford
Launceston
Tavy
Yes Tor
High Willhays
Moreton Hampstead
Starcross
Dawlish
Exmouth
Sidmouth
Lyme Bay
Dorchester
R. Frome
Wareham
Melcombe Regis
Weymouth
I. of Purbeck
Chesil Bank
Chesilton
Portland I.
Bill of Portland
St. Albans
Padstow
Brown Willy
Wadebridge
R. Camel
Bodmin
Callington
Dartmoor Forest
Tavistock
Newton Abbot
Ashburton
Teignmouth
Torquay
Paignton
Tor Bay
Brixham
Watergate B.
New Quay
CORNWALL
Lostwithiel
Liskeard
Saltash
Devonport
Plymouth
Totnes
Looe
Fowey
Dartmouth
Kingswear
R. Dart
Truro
St. Austell
St. Austell B.
Dodman Pt.
Plymouth Sound
Kingsbridge
Start B.
Start Pt.
Prawle Pt.
Eddystone Light Ho.
Falmouth B.
Manacles
Lizard Hd.

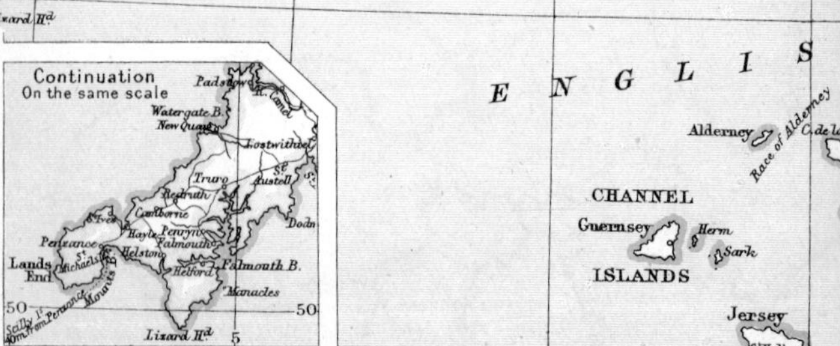

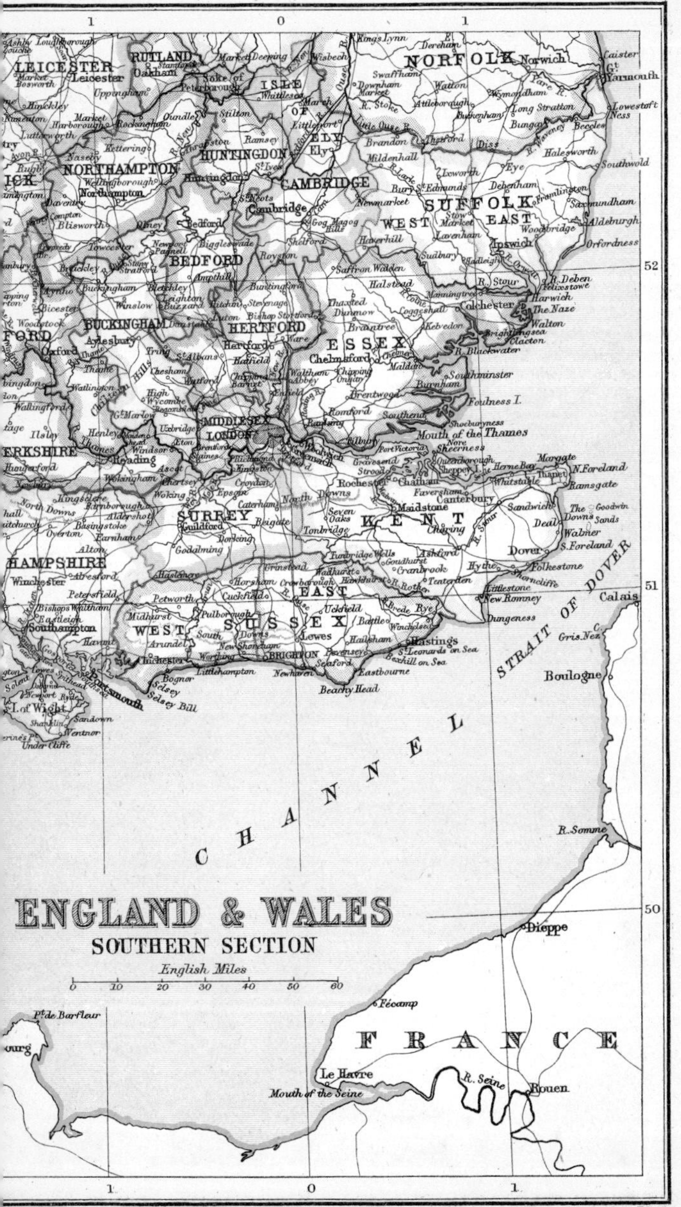

John Bartholomew & Co., Edinr.

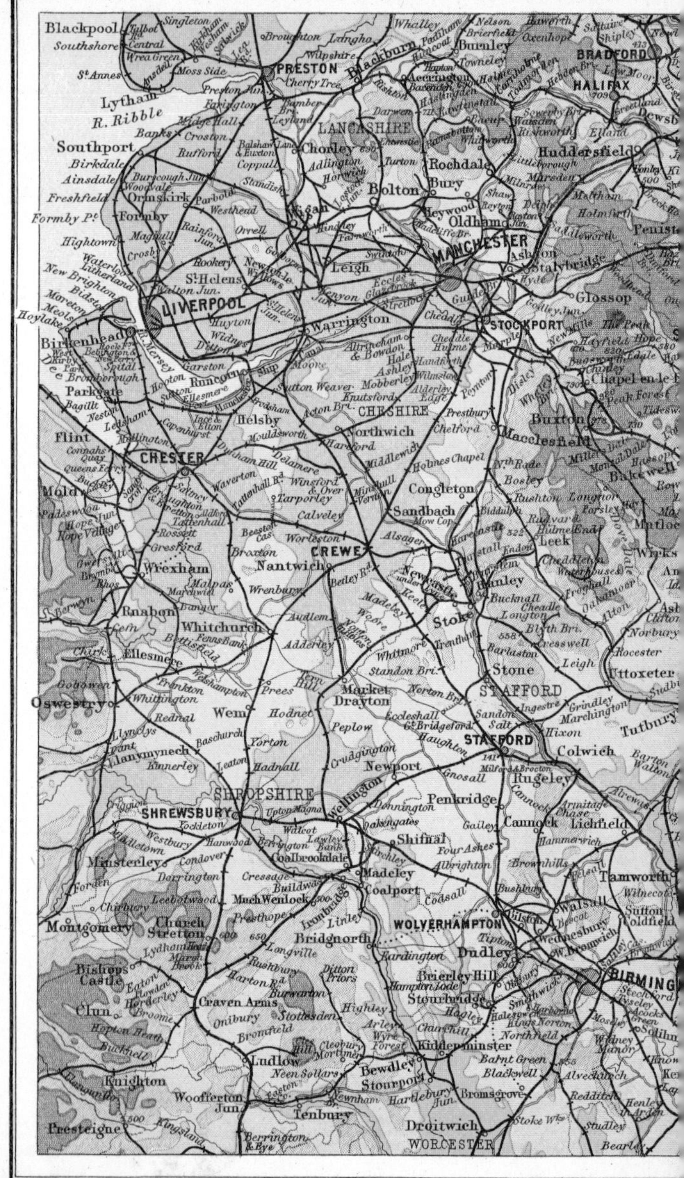
Blackpool
Preston
Blackburn
Burnley
Bradford
Halifax
Lytham
R. Ribble
Southport
Lancashire
Chorley
Rochdale
Huddersfield
Bolton
Ormskirk
Wigan
Oldham
Manchester
Leigh
St. Helens
Liverpool
Warrington
Stockport
Glossop
Birkenhead
Runcorn
Cheshire
Northwich
Chester
Macclesfield
Buxton
Congleton
Sandbach
Crewe
Nantwich
Wrexham
Leek
Ruabon
Whitchurch
Stoke
Ellesmere
Oswestry
Stone
Stafford
Market Drayton
Wem
Uttoxeter
Newport
Shropshire
Shrewsbury
Wellington
Rugeley
Lichfield
Cannock
Shifnal
Tamworth
Wolverhampton
Walsall
Montgomery
Church Stretton
Bridgnorth
Dudley
Birmingham
Bishops Castle
Craven Arms
Stourbridge
Kidderminster
Ludlow
Bewdley
Knighton
Tenbury
Droitwich
Presteigne
Worcester

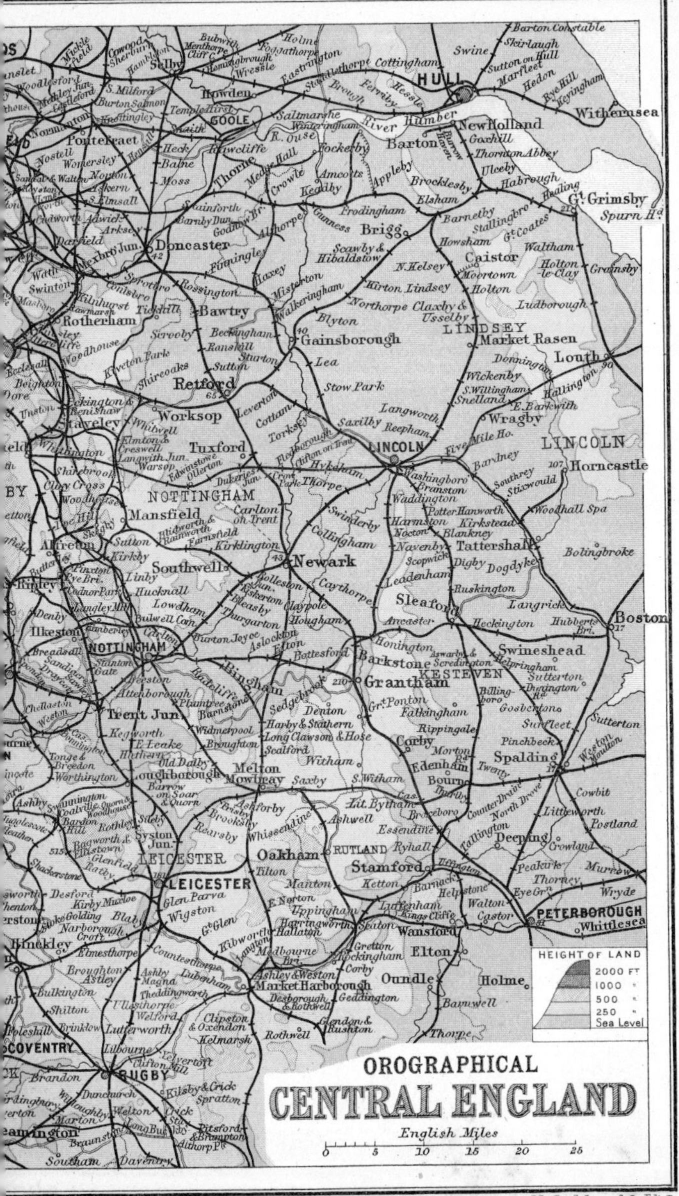

John Bartholomew & Co., Edinr.

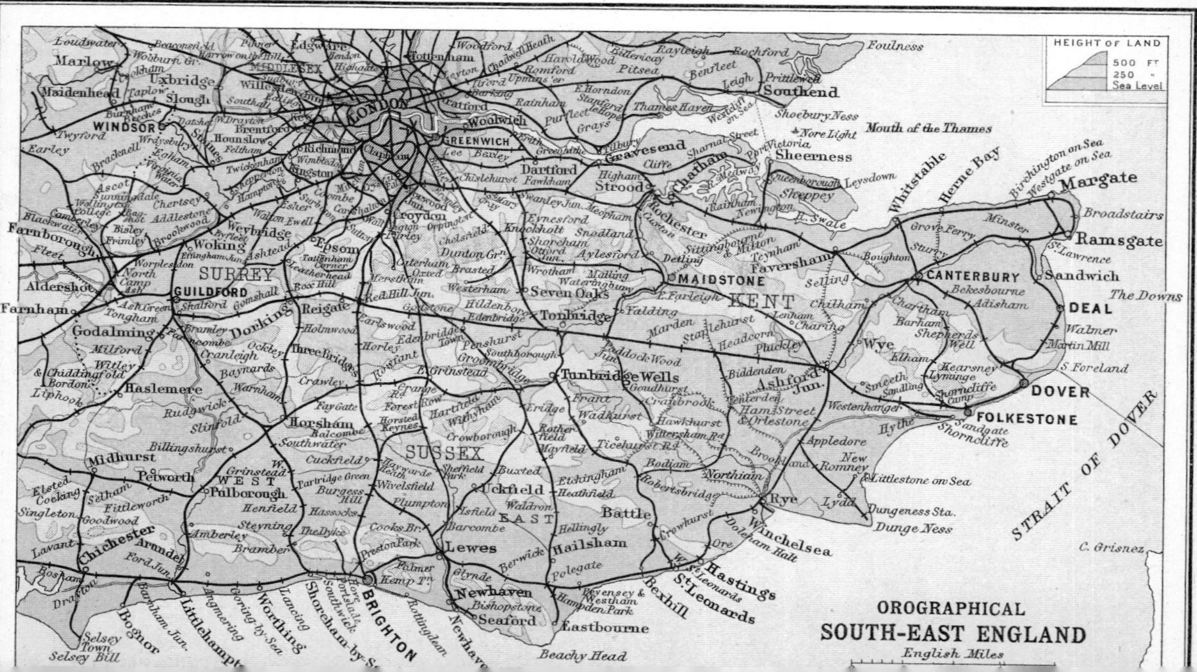
OROGRAPHICAL
SOUTH-EAST ENGLAND
English Miles
HEIGHT OF LAND
500 FT
250 "
Sea Level
STRAIT OF DOVER
Mouth of the Thames
The Downs
KENT
SURREY
SUSSEX
WEST
EAST
MIDDLESEX
LONDON
BRIGHTON
DOVER
FOLKESTONE
DEAL
CANTERBURY
MAIDSTONE
GUILDFORD
WINDSOR
GREENWICH
Margate
Ramsgate
Sandwich
Whitstable
Herne Bay
Sheerness
Southend
Gravesend
Chatham
Rochester
Strood
Dartford
Faversham
Ashford Jun.
Tunbridge Wells
Tonbridge
Seven Oaks
Reigate
Dorking
Epsom
Horsham
Haslemere
Godalming
Aldershot
Farnham
Farnborough
Woking
Weybridge
Croydon
Uxbridge
Slough
Maidenhead
Marlow
Chichester
Arundel
Bognor
Lancing
Worthing
Lewes
Newhaven
Seaford
Eastbourne
Beachy Head
Hailsham
Battle
Bexhill
St. Leonards
Hastings
Winchelsea
Rye
Dungeness Sta.
Dunge Ness
Hythe
C. Grisnez
S. Foreland
Foulness

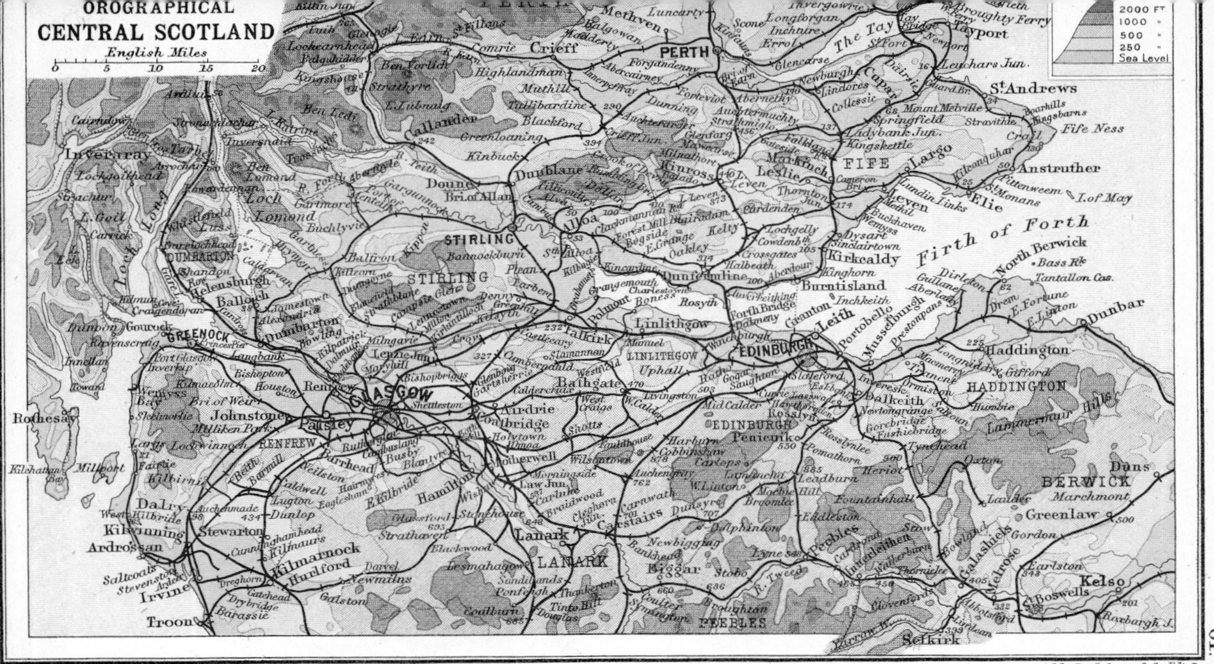

John Bartholomew & Co., Edin.

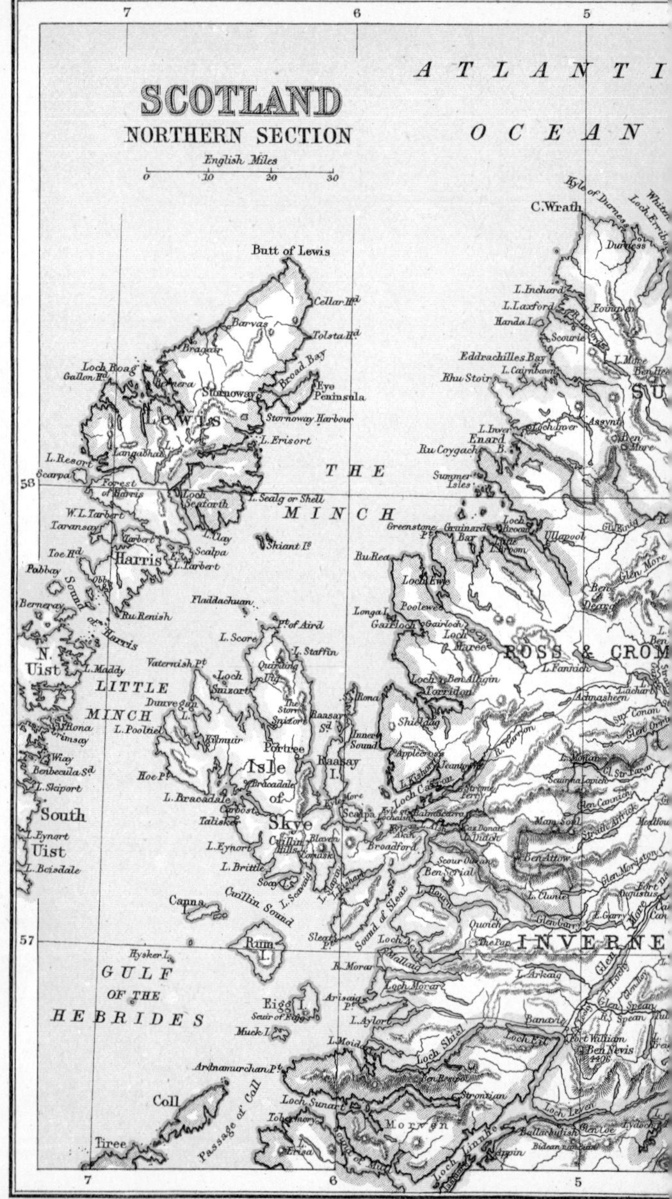
SCOTLAND
NORTHERN SECTION
English Miles
0 10 20 30
ATLANTIC
OCEAN
C. Wrath
Kyle of Durness
Durness
L. Inchard
L. Laxford
Handa I.
Scourie
Eddrachilles Bay
L. Cairnbawn
Rhu Stoir
L. More
Assynt
Ben More
L. Inver
Enard B.
Ru Coygach
Summer Isles
Loch Broom
Ullapool
Greenstone Pt.
Gruinard Bay
Ru Rea
Loch Ewe
Poolewe
Longa I.
Gairloch
Loch Maree
ROSS & CROM
L. Fannich
Achnasheen
Ben Alligin
Loch Torridon
Shieldag
Applecross
L. Kishorn
Loch Carron
Glen Cannich
Mam Soul
Ben Attow
Glen Moriston
Fort Augustus
L. Clunie
Glen Garry
L. Garry
Quoich
INVERNE
L. Arkaig
Glen Spean
Spean
Banavie
Fort William
Ben Nevis
Loch Eil
Loch Shiel
Ben Resipol
Strontian
Loch Leven
Ballachulish
Glen Coe
Appin
Loch Linnhe
Morven
Loch Sunart
Tobermory
Sound of Mull
Butt of Lewis
Cellar Hd.
Barvas
Tolsta Hd.
Bragar
Broad Bay
Loch Roag
Gallon Hd.
Stornoway
Eye Peninsula
Lewis
Stornoway Harbour
L. Erisort
L. Resort
Scarpa
Forest of Harris
Loch Seaforth
L. Sealg or Shell
THE
MINCH
W. L. Tarbert
Taransay
Tarbert
Toe Hd.
Harris
Scalpa
L. Tarbert
Shiant Is.
Pabbay
Sound of Harris
Berneray
Ru Renish
Fladdachuan
Pt. of Aird
L. Score
L. Staffin
N. Uist
L. Maddy
Vaternish Pt.
Loch Snizort
Quiraing
Uig
LITTLE
MINCH
Duvegan L.
L. Pooltiel
Rona
Grimsay
Kilmuir
Portree
Raasay Sd.
Inner Sound
Raasay I.
Wiay
Benbecula Sd.
Hoe Pt.
Isle of Skye
Bracadale
L. Bracadale
L. Skiport
South Uist
Carbost
Talisker
Scalpa
Broadford
L. Eynort
L. Boisdale
Cuillin Hills
Blaven
L. Brittle
Soay
L. Scavaig
Canna
Cuillin Sound
Sound of Sleat
Sleat Pt.
Loch Nevis
Mallaig
R. Morar
Loch Morar
Rum I.
Hysker I.
GULF
OF THE
HEBRIDES
Eigg I.
Scuir of Eigg
Arisaig Pt.
L. Aylort
Muck I.
L. Moidart
Ardnamurchan Pt.
Coll
Passage of Coll
Tiree
58
57
7
6
5

John Bartholomew & Co., Edinr.

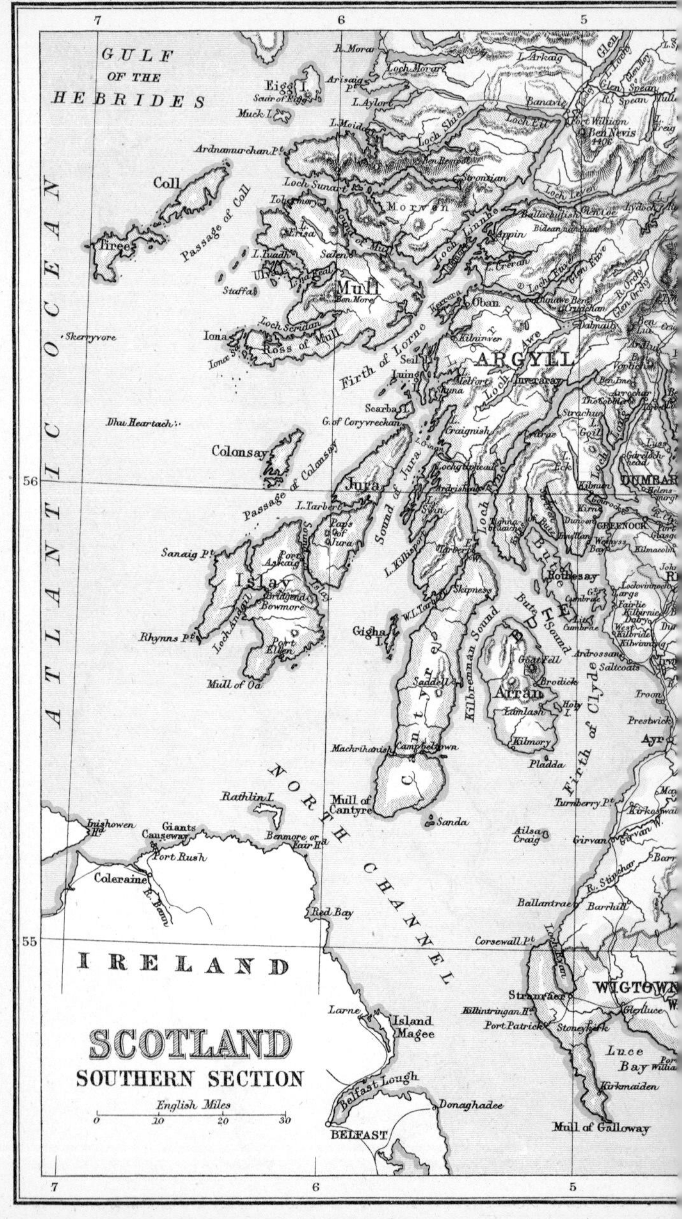
GULF OF THE HEBRIDES
ATLANTIC OCEAN
Coll
Tiree
Passage of Coll
Eigg I.
Muck I.
Ardnamurchan Pt.
Loch Sunart
Tobermory
Staffa
Mull
Ben More
Loch Seridan
Iona
Ross of Mull
Skerryvore
Firth of Lorne
Morven
Sound of Mull
Loch Linnhe
Loch Shiel
Loch Eil
Port William
Ben Nevis
Loch Leven
Appin
Oban
Loch Awe
Lorn
ARGYLL
Inveraray
Scarba I.
Luing
Seil I.
Dhu Heartach
Colonsay
Passage of Colonsay
G. of Coryvreckan
Jura
Paps of Jura
Sound of Jura
L. Tarbert
Sound of Islay
Sanaig Pt.
Islay
Port Askaig
Bridgend
Bowmore
Port Ellen
Rhynns Pt.
Mull of Oa
Gigha I.
Kilbrennan Sound
Cantyre
Saddell
Campbeltown
Machrihanish
Mull of Cantyre
Sanda
Loch Fyne
Bute
Rothesay
Arran
Goat Fell
Brodick
Lamlash
Holy I.
Kilmory
Pladda
Firth of Clyde
GREENOCK
Ardrossan
Saltcoats
Troon
Prestwick
Ayr
Turnberry Pt.
Ailsa Craig
Girvan
Ballantrae
Barrhill
Corsewall Pt.
Stranraer
Killintringan Hd.
Port Patrick
Stoneykirk
Luce Bay
Kirkmaiden
Mull of Galloway
WIGTOWN
Rathlin I.
NORTH CHANNEL
Inishowen Hd.
Giants Causeway
Port Rush
Coleraine
R. Bann
Benmore or Fair Hd.
Red Bay
IRELAND
Larne
Island Magee
Belfast Lough
Donaghadee
BELFAST
SCOTLAND
SOUTHERN SECTION
English Miles
0 10 20 30
7
6
5
56
55

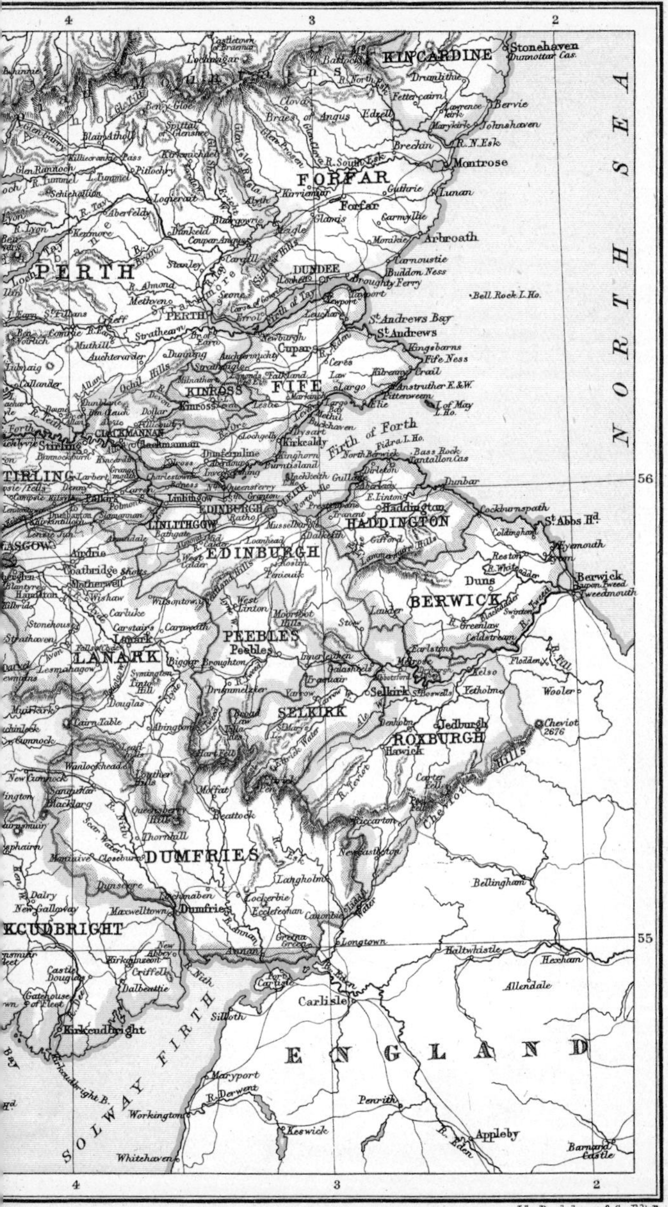

John Bartholomew & Co., Edinr.

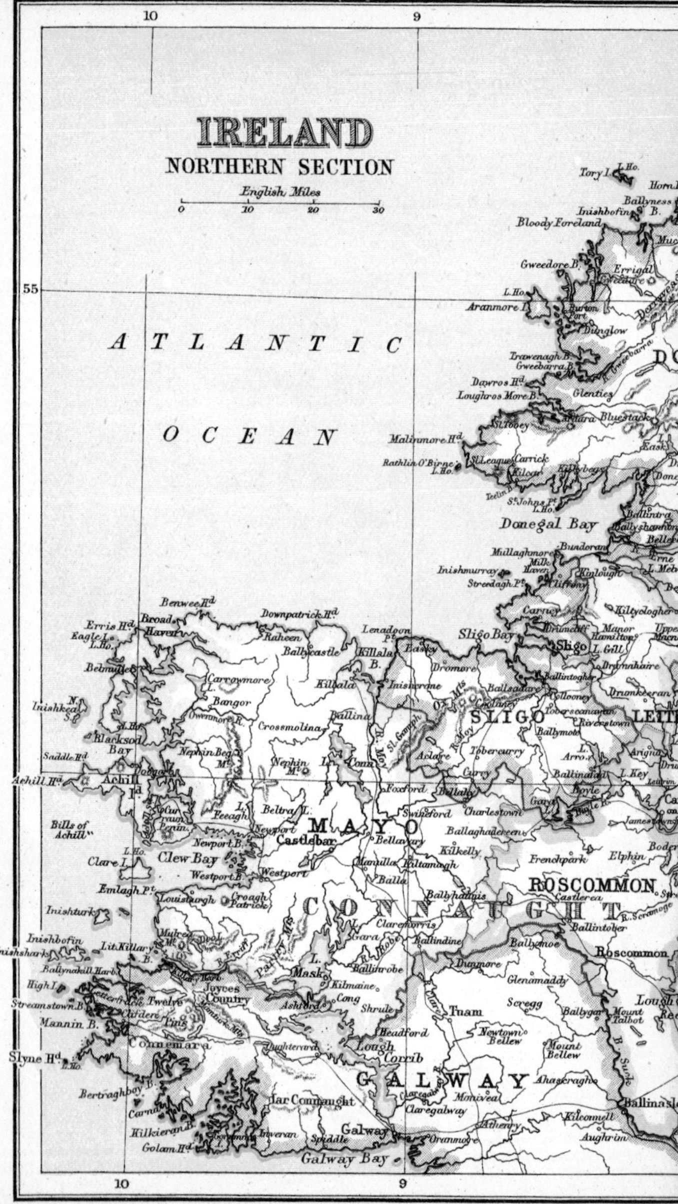
IRELAND
NORTHERN SECTION
English Miles
ATLANTIC
OCEAN
MAYO
SLIGO
CONNAUGHT
ROSCOMMON
GALWAY
Donegal Bay
Sligo Bay
Clew Bay
Galway Bay
Bloody Foreland
Tory I.
Achill Hd.
Achill Id.
Slyne Hd.
Castlebar
Sligo
Galway
Roscommon
Westport
Ballina
Tuam
Connemara
Lough Corrib
L. Mask
Joyces Country
Twelve Pins
Clare I.
Inishturk
Inishbofin
Downpatrick Hd.
Benwee Hd.
Erris Hd.
Blacksod Bay
Belmullet
Crossmolina
Swineford
Claremorris
Ballinrobe
Ballinasloe

John Bartholomew & Co., Edinr.

10
9
53
52
ATLANTIC OCEAN
GALWAY
CLARE
LIMERICK
KERRY
CORK
MUNST
Ballynakill Harb.
High I.
Streamstown B.
Mannin B.
Slyne Hd.
L. Ho.
Bertraghboy B.
Kilkieran B.
Golam Hd.
North Sound
Joyces Country
Connemara
Clifden
Mask
Ballinrobe
Kilmaine
Cong
Ashford
Shrule
Tuam
Glenamaddy
Seregg
Ballygar
Headford
Newtown Bellew
Mount Bellew
Oughterard
Lough Corrib
Iar Connaught
Monivea
Claregalway
Ahascragh
Kilconnell
Athenry
Aughrim
Galway
Oranmore
Spiddle
Craughwell
Loughrea
Galway Bay
Black Hd.
Ardrahan
Killimor
Kinvarra
Aran Islands
Inishmore
Inishmaan
Inisheer
South Sound
Ballyvaghan
Slieve Aughty Mts.
Woodford
Gort
Lisdoonvarna
Cliffs of Moher
Kilfenora
Corrofin
Liscannor
Lough
Hags Hd.
Liscannor B.
Ennistimon
Crusheen
Scarriff
Mal Bay
Milltown Malbay
Ennis
Tulla
Nenagh
Mutton I.
Clare
Killaloe
Ballina
Killard Pt.
Newmarket
Sixmilebridge
Castleconnell
Newport
Doonbeg
Kilkee B.
Kilkee
Shannon
Kilrush
Killadysert
LIMERICK
Pallaskenry
Scattery I.
Foynes
Askeaton
Caherconlish
Loop Hd.
Tarbert
Glin
Adare
Pallas Grean
Ballylongford
Ballyhahill
Rathkeale
Croom
River Shannon
R. Cashen
Ballybunnion
Bruff
Hospital
Listowel
Ballingarry
Kerry Hd.
R. Feale
Newcastle
Bruree
Kilmallock
Ballyheige B.
R. Deel
Ballylanders
Ardfert
Abbeyfeale
Dromcolliher
Charleville
Kilfinnane
Brandon Bay
Brandon Hd.
Tralee B.
Tralee
Castleisland
Sybil Hd.
Brandon Hills
Castlegregory
Slieve Mish
Buttevant
R. Sheep
Smerwick Harb.
Newmarket
Doneraile
Dunmore Hd.
Dingle
Castlemaine
R. Maine
Kanturk
Blasket I.
Slea Hd.
Boherboy
R. Blackwater
Mallow
Killorglin
Banteer
Rathcormack
Dingle Bay
Glenbeigh
Killarney
L. Leane
Millstreet
Boggagh Mts.
Macgillicuddys Reeks
Carrantual
Watergrass
Valencia Harb.
Mangerton
Donoughmore
Cahirciveen
Valencia I.
Bray Hd.
Derrynasaggart Mts.
Kilgarvan
Coachford
Blarney
CORK
Portmagee
R. Inny
Kenmare
R. Roughty
Macroom
R. Lee
L. Currane
Sneem
Inchigeelagh
Ballincollig
Passage West
Bolus Hd.
Waterville
L. Allua
Ballinskelligs B.
Caha Mts.
Crosshaven
Scariff I.
Lambs Hd.
Kenmare River
Glengarriff
Keakill
Dunmanway
Ballyneen
Bandon
Innishannon
Hungry Hill
R. Bandon
Kinsale
Bantry
Kilbrittain
Drimoleague
Kinsale Harb.
Dursey I.
Bere I.
Clonakilty
Bull Rk.
L. Ho.
Crow Hd.
Bantry Bay
Ross Carbery
Old Head of Ki
Ballydehob
Courtmacsherry B.
Sheep Hd.
Dunmanus Bay
Skull
Skibbereen
Clonakilty B.
Seven Heads
Mizen Hd.
Roaring Water B.
Baltimore
Toe Hd.
Galley Hd. L. Ho.
Rosscarbery B.
Crookhaven
Sherkin I.
Clear I.
Cape Clear
Fastnet Lt. Ho.

John Bartholomew & Co, Edin.

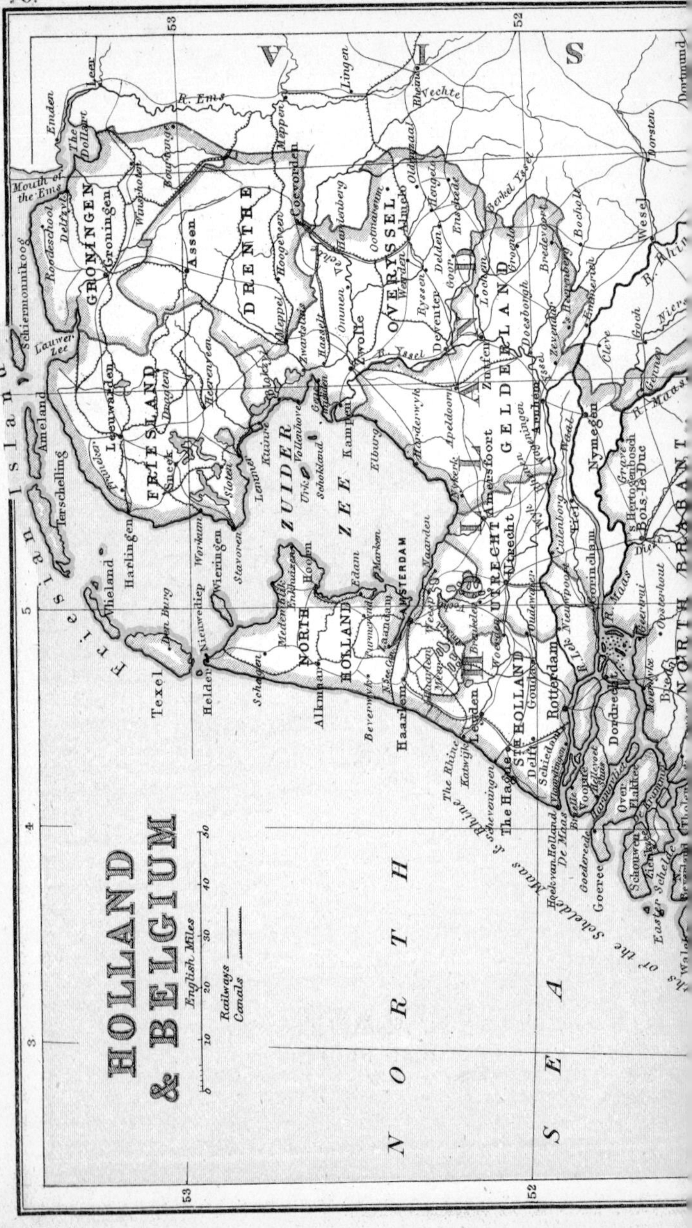

HOLLAND & BELGIUM

English Miles

0 10 20 30 40 50

Railways
Canals

NORTH SEA

Friesian Islands
Schiermonnikoog
Ameland
Terschelling
Vlieland
Texel
Den Burg
Helder
Nieuwediep
Wieringen
Harlingen
Workum
Stavoren
Lauwer Zee
Mouth of the Ems
The Dollart
Emden
Leer
R. Ems
Roodeschool
Delfzyl
GRONINGEN
Groningen
Winschoten
Bourtange
FRIESLAND
Franeker
Leeuwarden
Sneek
Dragten
Heerenveen
Sloten
Lemmer
Kuinre
Blokzyl
Assen
DRENTHE
Meppel
Hoogeveen
Meppen
Coevorden
Lingen
ZUIDER ZEE
Urk
Vollenhove
Schokland
Genemuiden
Zwartsluis
Hasselt
Kampen
Elburg
Zwolle
Ommen
Vechte
Hardenberg
Ootmarsum
OVERYSSEL
Wierden
Almelo
Oldenzaal
Rheine
Ryssen
Hengelo
Deventer
Delden
Goor
Enschede
NORTH HOLLAND
Schagen
Medemblik
Enkhuizen
Hoorn
Alkmaar
Edam
Beverwyk
Purmerend
Marken
N. Sea Can.
Zaandam
Haarlem
AMSTERDAM
Naarden
Harderwyk
Haarlem Meer
Weesp
Nykerk
Apeldoorn
The Rhine
Katwyk
Leyden
Breukelen
HOLLAND
Amersfoort
Zutfen
Lochem
Scheveningen
The Hague
Woerden
UTRECHT
Utrecht
GELDERLAND
Groenlo
Berkel Yssel
STH HOLLAND
Delft
Gouda
Oudewater
Wyk
Rhenen
Wageningen
Arnhem
Yssel
Doesborgh
Schiedam
Rotterdam
Vlaardingen
Hoek van Holland
De Maas
Maas & Rhine
Mouths of the Schelde
Brielle
Voorne
Hellevoet Sluis
Goedereede
Goeree
R. Lek
Nieuwpoort
Culenborg
Tiel
Waal
Zevenaar
's Heerenberg
Bredevoort
Bocholt
Emmerich
Gorincham
Nymegen
Cleve
Dordrecht
R. Maas
Grave
's Hertogenbosch
Bois-le-Duc
Dieze
Schouwen
Zierikzee
Over Flakkee
Haringvliet
De Krammer
Geertrui
Moerdyke
Oosterhout
Breda
Easter Schelde
NORTH BRABANT
Goch
Gennep
Niers
R. Rhine
Wesel
Dorsten
Dortmund

BELGIUM
FRANCE
PRUSSIA
WEST FLANDERS
EAST FLANDERS
ANTWERP
LIMBURG
LIM-BURG
BRABANT
HAINAUT
NAMUR
LIEGE
LUXEMBURG
LUXEMBURG
Ardennes
Zeebrugge
Blankenberghe
Heyst
Yzendyke
Neuzen
Hulst
Sas van Gent
Ostende
Damme
Bruges
Eecloo
Nieuport
Thourout
Veurne
Dixmude
Thielt
Roulers
Iseghem
Poperinghe
Ypres
Courtrai
Menin
Tourcoing
Roubaix
Lille
Gand
Lokeren
Wetteren
Termonde
St. Nicolas
Alost
Oudenarde
Renaix
Grammont
Lessines
Enghien
Ath
Leuze
Tournai
Peruwelz
Turnhout
Antwerp
Boom
Lierre
R. Nethe
Gheel
Mechlin
Aerschot
Diest
Maaseyk
Hasselt
Tongres
St. Trond
Maastricht
Louvain
Tirlemont
BRUSSELS
Hal
Waterloo
Waveren
La Belle Alliance
Braine le Comte
Genappe
Quatre Bras
Nivelles
Soignies
Gembloux
Namur
Mons
Jemappes
Wasmes
Dour
Charleroi
Chatelet
Thuin
Beaumont
Philippeville
Marienbourg
Chimay
Couvin
Dinant
Jemelle
Marche
la Roche
Durbuy
Liege
Seraing
Huy
Herve
Eupen
Verviers
Spa
Stavelot
Amblève
Hourfalize
Bastogne
St. Hubert
Givet
Fumay
Rocroy
Hirson
Charleville
Mezières
Sedan
Neufchâteau
Martelange
Bouillon
Chiny
Arlon
Virton
Longwy
Esch
Luxemburg
Mersch
Fels
Diekirch
Wilz
Vianden
Clerf
Treves
St. Amand
Douai
Valenciennes
Arras
Cambrai
Venlo
Crefeld
Viersen
Roermonde
Weert
Elberfeld
Barmen
Hagen
Düsseldorf
Cologne
Düren
Aix la Chapelle
Bonn
Escaut
Scheldt
Lys
Dender
Senne
Dyle
Thil
Rupel
Sambre
Meuse
Ourthe
Vesdre
Lesse
R. Semoy
Oise
Aisne
Maas
R. Roer
R. Rhine
Moselle
Sauer
Our
3
4
5
7
50
51
John Bartholomew & Co., Edinr.

FRANCE
English Miles
0 20 40 60 80 100
ENGLAND
ENGLISH CHANNEL
ATLANTIC OCEAN
BAY OF BISCAY
SPAIN
I. of Wight
Lands End
Scilly Is.
Lizard Hd.
Channel Islands (to England)
Guernsey
Sark
Alderney
Jersey
C. de la Hague
Cherbourg
Havre
Dieppe
Fécamp
Trouville
Honfleur
Caen
CALVADOS
Falaise
Lizieux
St. Lo
Coutances
Granville
Cancale
St. Malo
Avranches
MANCHE
SEINE INFÉR.
EURE
Evreux
Elbeuf
Louviers
Laigle
ORNE
Alençon
Séez
Ushant I.
Pt. St. Matthieu
Brest
Morlaix
Guingamp
St. Brieuc
Dinan
St. Servan
FINISTÈRE
COTES DU NORD
Douarnenez B.
Quimper
Pontivy
MORBIHAN
Vannes
Lorient
I. Croix
Morbihan B.
Belle Isle
ILLE ET VILAINE
Rennes
Vitré
Fougères
MAYENNE
Mayenne
Laval
SARTHE
Le Mans
La Fleche
Vendôme
Chateaubriant
MAINE ET LOIRE
Angers
Saumur
Cholet
LOIRE INFÉRIEURE
Nantes
St. Nazaire
R. Loire
Paimbœuf
I. Noirmoutier
I. Dieu
Tours
Blois
INDRE ET LOIRE
Chinon
La Roche sur Yonne (Vendée)
VENDÉE
Sables d'Olonne
Fontenay le Comte
DEUX SÈVRES
Niort
Châtellerault
Poitiers
VIENNE
I. de Ré
La Rochelle
R. Charente
Rochefort
I. d'Oléron
CHARENTE INFÉRre
Saintes
Royan
CHARENTE
Cognac
Angoulême
R. Gironde
Pauillac
Medoc
Blaye
Bordeaux
Libourne
Bergerac
DORDOGNE
Perigueux
Basin d'Arcachon
La Teste de Buch
GIRONDE
R. Garonne
LOT ET GARONNE
Agen
LANDES
Mont de Marsan
Dax
Condom
Lectoure
Auch
GERS
Biarritz
Bayonne
R. Adour
Pau
BASSES PYRENEES
Oloron
Tarbes
Bigorre
HAUTES PYRENEES
Luz
Luchon
Mt. Perdu
Mt. Maladetta
Herblay
Ermont
Enghien
Gonesse
Montmorency
Franconville
Pierrefitte
Arnouville
Maison
Argenteuil
Epinay
Stains
Dugny
Poissy
Gennevilliers
St. Denis
le Bourget
Bezons
Colombes
Aubervilliers
Asnières
St. Ouen
Courbevoie
Ourcq
Bondy
Chatou
Nanterre
S. Germain
Neuilly
Passy
Romainville
Belleville
Bagnolet
Rosny
Marly
Malmaison
Suresnes
Longchamp
PARIS
Montreuil
Vincennes
Boulogne
St. Cloud
Sèvres
Fontenay
Nogent
Vaugirard
S. Mandé
Charenton
Meudon
Trianon
Palaces
St. Cyr
VERSAILLES
Chatillon
Fontenai
Arcueil
Bicetre
Vitry
Ivry
Maisons
Villejuif
Creteil
Sceaux
Bourg
Choisy
Sucy
Chatenay
Bonneuil
Miles
0 2 4

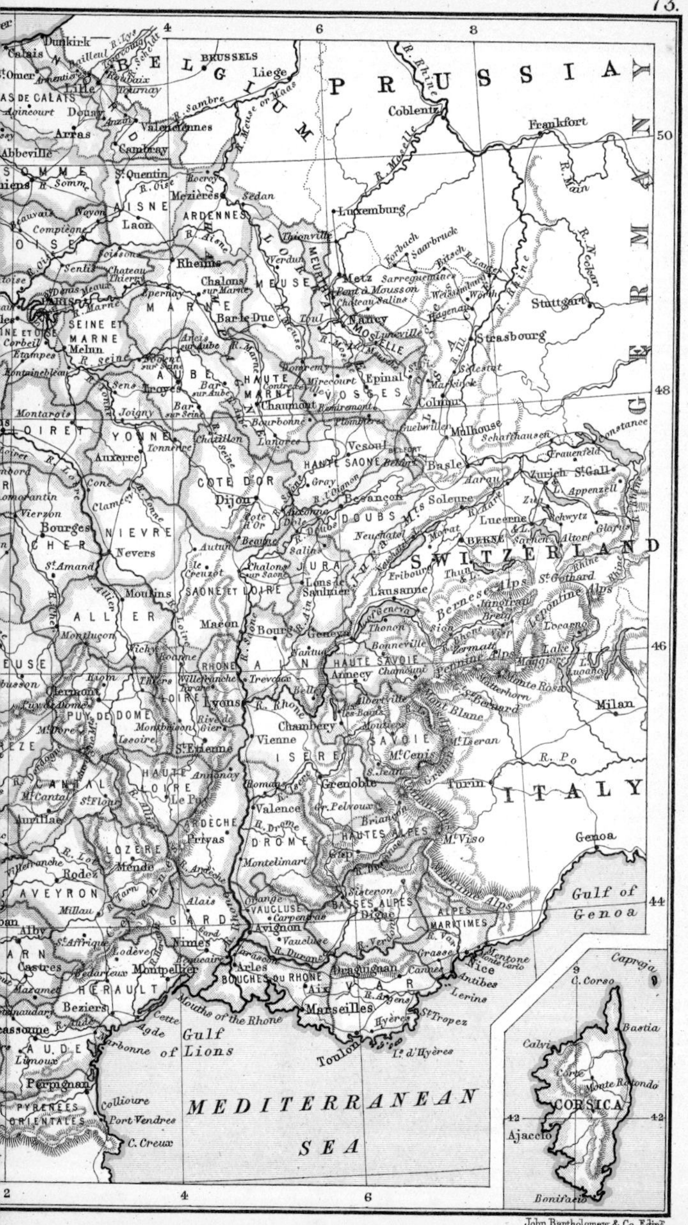
PRUSSIA
BELGIUM
BRUSSELS
SWITZERLAND
ITALY
MEDITERRANEAN SEA
Gulf of Lions
Gulf of Genoa
CORSICA
John Bartholomew & Co., Edin.r

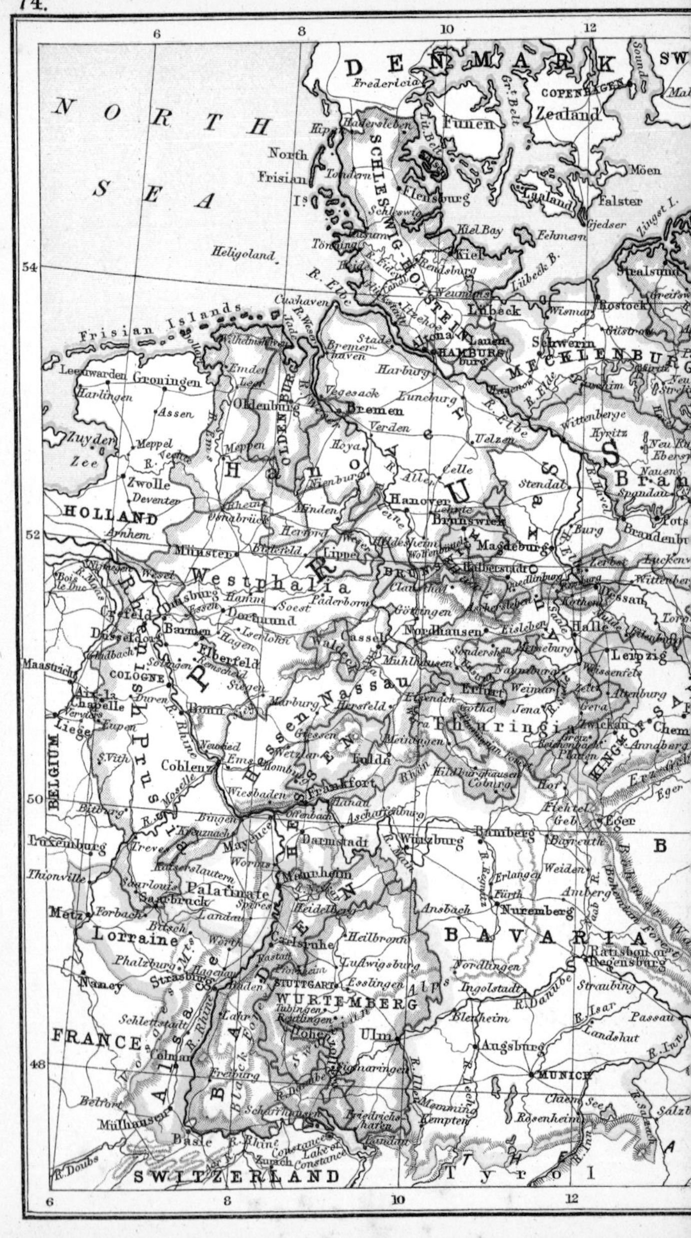
NORTH SEA
DENMARK
Funen
Zealand
COPENHAGEN
Laaland
Falster
Möen
Fehmern
North Frisian Is.
Heligoland
Frisian Islands
SCHLESWIG-HOLSTEIN
Flensburg
Kiel
Lübeck
HAMBURG
Altona
Bremen
MECKLENBURG
Schwerin
Rostock
Stralsund
Hanover
Brunswick
Magdeburg
HOLLAND
Groningen
Zwolle
Zuyder Zee
Amsterdam
Arnhem
Westphalia
Münster
Duisburg
Dortmund
Barmen
Elberfeld
Düsseldorf
COLOGNE
Bonn
Aix la Chapelle
Liege
Maastricht
BELGIUM
Coblentz
Rhenish Prussia
Hessen Nassau
Cassel
Frankfort
Wiesbaden
Mayence
Darmstadt
Mannheim
Heidelberg
Thuringia
Erfurt
Weimar
Jena
Leipzig
Halle
Dessau
Saxony
Luxemburg
Metz
Lorraine
Strasburg
Alsace
Carlsruhe
Stuttgart
WURTEMBERG
Ulm
Baden
Black Forest
Freiburg
Mülhausen
Basle
Constance
Lake of Constance
Zurich
SWITZERLAND
BAVARIA
Nuremberg
Bamberg
Würzburg
Augsburg
MUNICH
Ratisbon or Regensburg
Passau
Palatinate
FRANCE
Nancy
Tyrol
Brandenburg
6
8
10
12
54
52
50
48

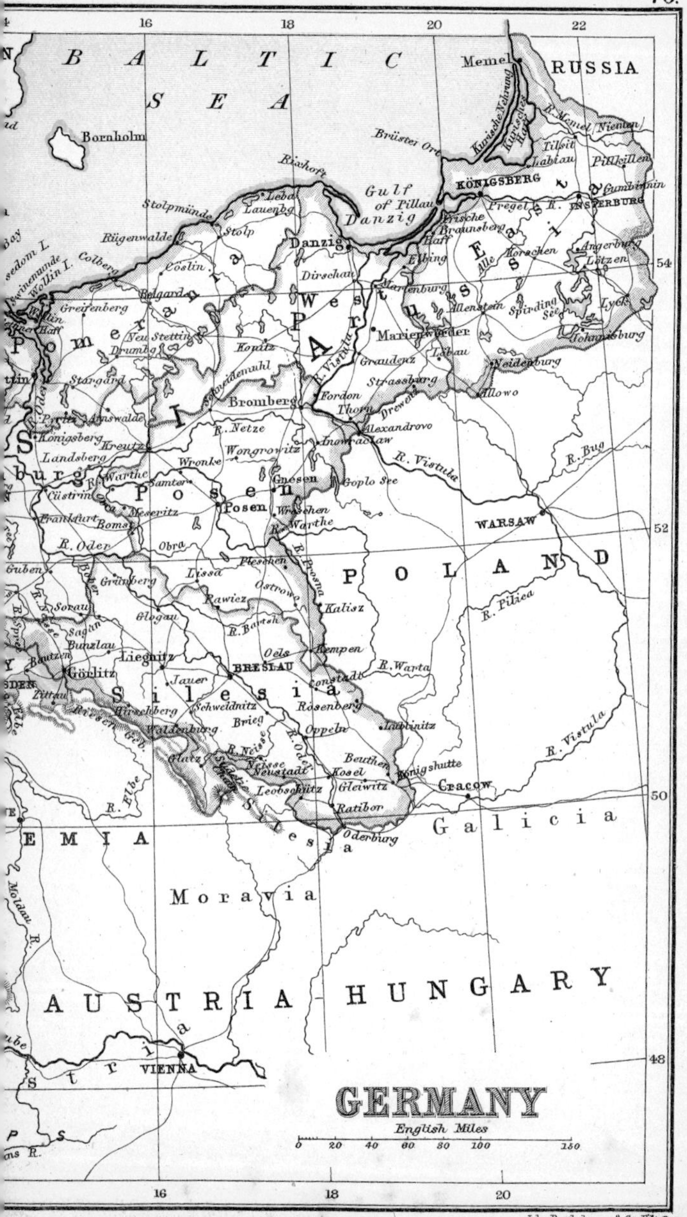

John Bartholomew & Co., Edinr.

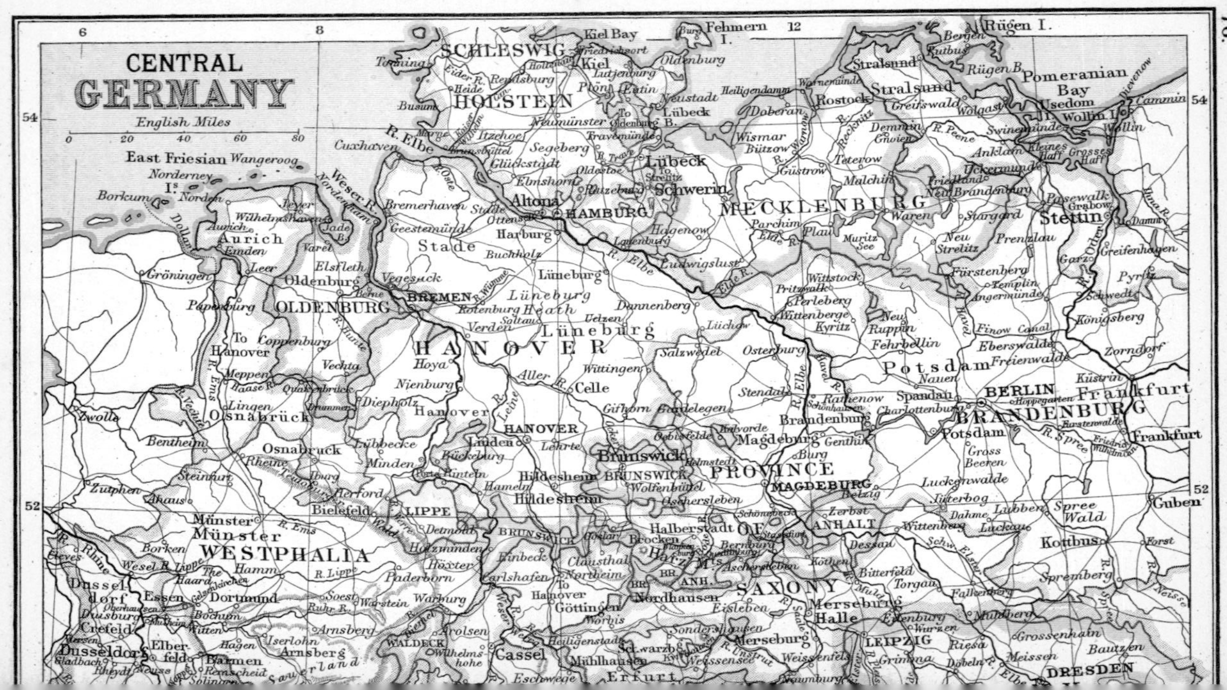
CENTRAL
GERMANY
English Miles
0 20 40 60 80
East Friesian Is.
SCHLESWIG
HOLSTEIN
MECKLENBURG
HANOVER
OLDENBURG
WESTPHALIA
BRANDENBURG
PROVINCE OF SAXONY
ANHALT
BRUNSWICK
LIPPE
WALDECK
BERLIN
HAMBURG
BREMEN
MAGDEBURG
LEIPZIG
DRESDEN
Pomeranian Bay
Kiel Bay
Rügen I.
Fehmern I.

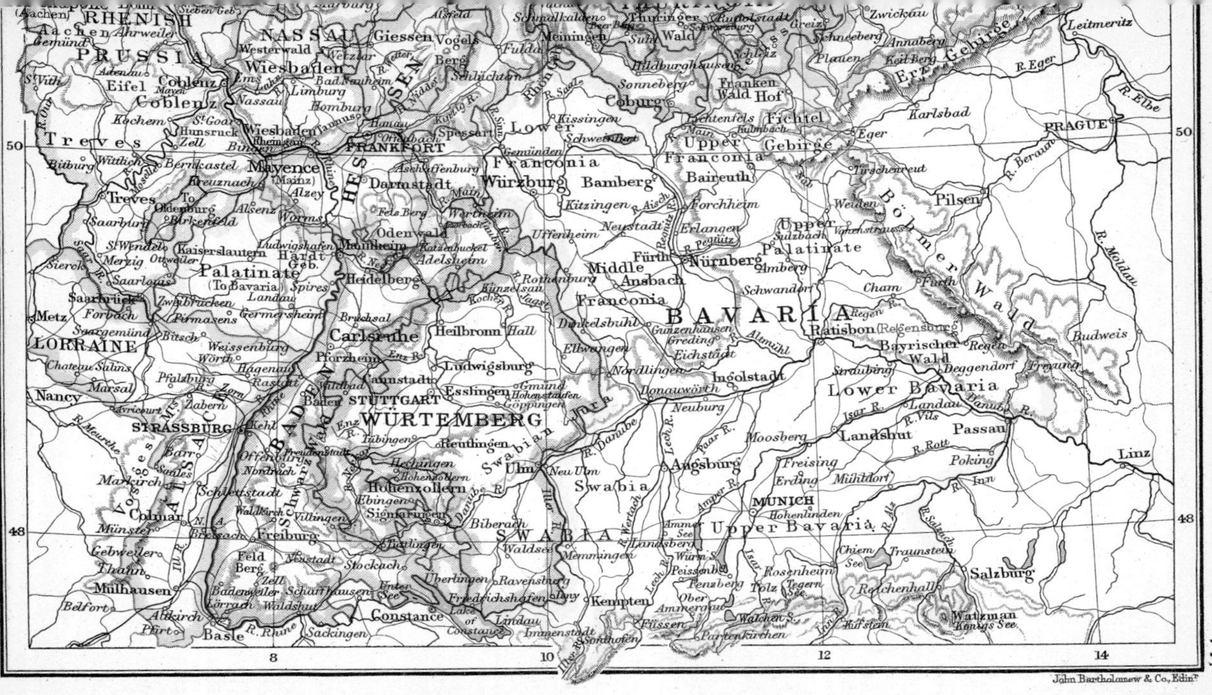
RHENISH PRUSSIA
NASSAU
HESSEN
BADEN
WÜRTEMBERG
BAVARIA
Palatinate (To Bavaria)
LORRAINE
ALSACE
Hohenzollern
Upper Bavaria
Lower Bavaria
Upper Palatinate
Upper Franconia
Middle Franconia
Lower Franconia
Swabia
Swabian Jura
PRAGUE
MUNICH
FRANKFORT
STUTTGART
STRASSBURG
Carlsruhe
Mayence (Mainz)
Wiesbaden
Coblenz
Treves
Metz
Nancy
Basle
Constance
Lake of Constance
Ulm
Augsburg
Nürnberg
Ratisbon (Regensburg)
Passau
Salzburg
Linz
Pilsen
Budweis
Eger
Karlsbad
Würzburg
Bamberg
Baireuth
Darmstadt
Heidelberg
Freiburg
Colmar
Mulhausen
Böhmer Wald
Bayrischer Wald
Schwarz Wald
Fichtel Gebirge
Erz Gebirge
R. Moldau
R. Elbe
Rhine
Danube
Isar R.
R. Inn
Lech R.
50
48
8
10
12
14
John Bartholomew & Co., Edin.r

10
12
14
16
50
48
46
44
G E R M A N
SAXONY
Dresden
Breslau
Erz Gebirge
Reichenberg
Schnee Koppe
Leitmeritz
Trautenau
Joachimsthal
Saaz
Jung Bunzlau
Melnik
Sadowa
Königgrätz
Glatz
Karlsbad
Eger
Prague
R. Elbe
Smichow
Pardubitz
Kolin
Kuttenberg
Bamberg
Marienbad
BOHEMIA
Pilsen
Pribram
Sternberg
Nurnburg
BAVARIA
Klattau
Deutsch Brod
Olmütz
Polna
Prossnitz
Pisek
Tabor
Iglau
MORAVIA
Schuttenhofen
Neuhaus
Brünn
Regensburg
Moravian Plateau
Austerlitz
Budweis
Wittingau
Eibenschitz
R. Danube
Krumau
Gmünd
Znaim
Nikolsburg
Isar
Passau
Sigmundsherberg
Augsburg
MUNICH
Braunau
Freystadt
UPPER
LOWER
Krems
R. Inn
Linz
Danube
VIENNA
Korn neuburg
Ried
Amstetten
St. Pölten
Pressburg
AUSTRIA
L. of Constance
R. Lech
Steyer
Gmunden
Scheibbs
Baden
Salzburg
Weyer
Neustadt
Wieselburg
Neusiedler See
Bregenz
Dornbirn
Kufstein
Wörgl
Ischl
Oedenburg
Feldkirch
R. Inn
Kitzbühel
SALZBURG
Steinach
Bludenz
Arlberg
Innsbruck
Gastein
Tauern Chain
Bruck
Vorarlberg
TYROL
High Tauern
Leoben
Güns
Papa
Judenburg
Steinamanger
Sterzing
Engadin
STYRIA
Graz
Veszprim
Stelvio P.
Brixen
Ortler
Meran
Sillian
CARINTHIA
Leibnitz
Bozen
Villach
Klagenfurt
Marburg
R. Mur
Mt. Adamello
Mt. Marmolade
Pettau
Gr. Kanizsa
R. Drave
Kaposvar
Belluno
Karawanken
Cilli
46
Trent
Udine
Laibach
Krapina
Warasdin
Riva
R. Etsch
Rovereto
Göritz
GÖRITZ
CARNIOLA
Littay
Gurkfeld
Kreuz
L. di Garda
Treviso
Trieste
Adelsberg
Gottschee
R. Save
Agram
Verona
Pirano
VENETIA
Padua
Venice
ISTRIA
Fiume
Karlstadt
Kulpa
Sissek
Pakracz
Adige
Abbazia
Buccari
CROATIA
Ogulin
R. Po
Rovigno
Veglia
Zeng
Sluin
R. Unna
Novi
Pola
Quarnero
Ottochatz
Bihac
R. Verbas
Bologna
ADRIATIC SEA
Gospich
Banialuka
Kliutch
Melada
Yaitze
Travnik
Zara
Lunga
Benkovaz
Mt. Dinara
Pisa
DALMATIA
Kupres
Livno
Incoronata
Dinaric Alps
Sebenico
Ancona
Zuri
Spalato
ITALY
Pta. della Planca
Brazza
Lissa
Lesina
S. Andrea
Tiber
Curzola
Lagosta
Meleda
12
14
16

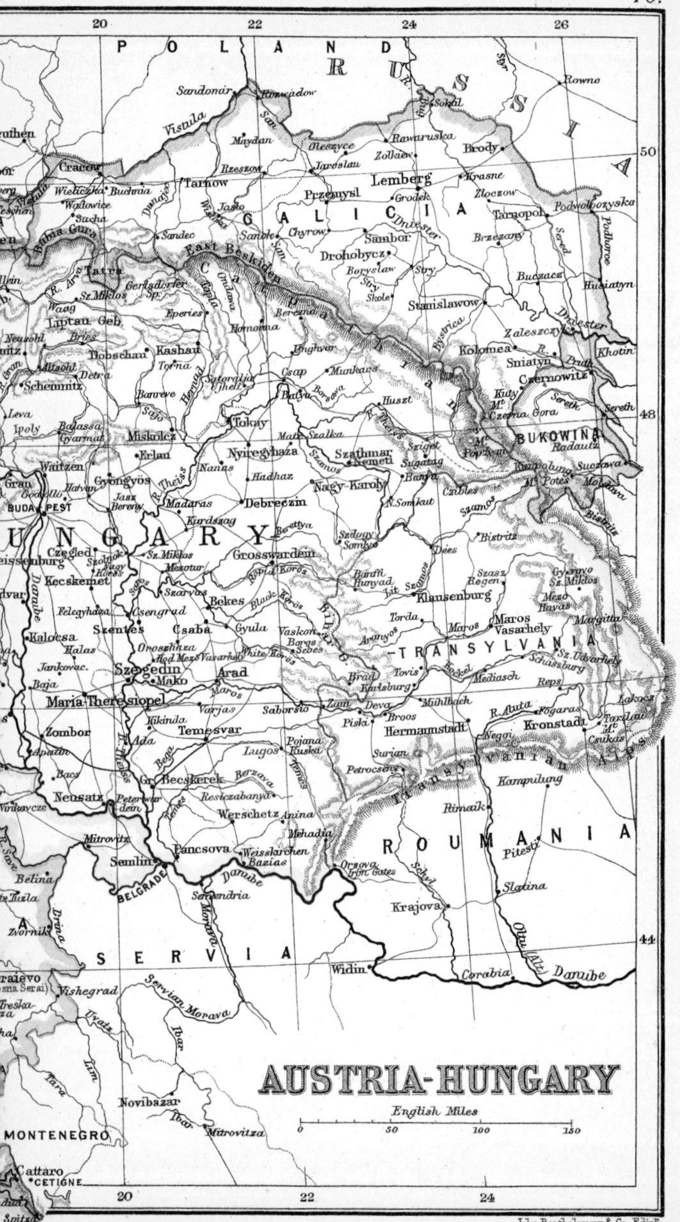
AUSTRIA-HUNGARY
English Miles
0 50 100 150
POLAND
RUSSIA
GALICIA
HUNGARY
TRANSYLVANIA
BUKOWINA
ROUMANIA
SERVIA
MONTENEGRO
Lemberg
Cracow
Debreczin
Klausenburg
Temesvar
Szegedin
BUDA PEST
BELGRADE
Hermannstadt
Kronstadt
Czernowitz
Transylvanian Alps
East Beskiden
Danube

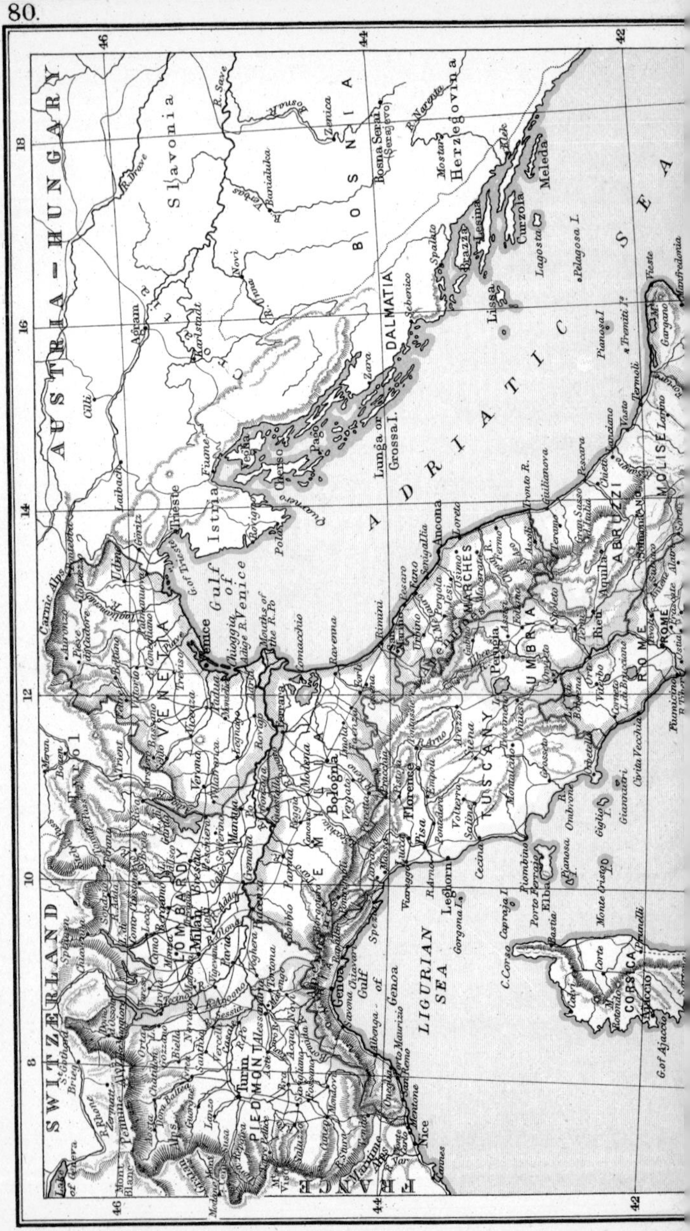

8 10 12 14 16 18

SWITZERLAND

AUSTRIA – HUNGARY

Tyrol

Slavonia

Croatia

BOSNIA

Herzegovina

DALMATIA

Istria

FRANCE

PIEDMONT

LOMBARDY

VENETIA

EMILIA

TUSCANY

MARCHES

UMBRIA

ABRUZZI

MOLISE

ROME

CORSICA

LIGURIAN SEA

Gulf of Genoa

Gulf of Venice

ADRIATIC SEA

Turin

Milan

Genoa

Venice

Bologna

Florence

Pisa

Leghorn

Perugia

Ancona

Trieste

Fiume

Agram

Bosna Serai (Serajevo)

Nice

46 44 42

ITALY
English Miles
0 10 20 40 60 80 100
TYRHENIAN SEA
MEDITERRANEAN SEA
IONIAN SEA
GULF OF TARANTO
APULIA
CAMPANIA
BASILICATA
CALABRIA
SICILY
SARDINIA
Naples
Brindisi
Monopoli
Taranto
Lecce
Otranto
Gallipoli
C.S.Maria di Leuca
Potenza
Salerno
Capri I.
Ischia
Pontine Is.
Ponza
Ventoteni
Cosenza
Catanzaro
Reggio
Strait of Messina
Messina
Palermo
Catania
Syracuse
Marsala
Trapani
Lipari Islands
Stromboli
Ustica
Ægades Is.
Pantellaria I.
Cagliari
Sassari
Nuoro
Oristano
Porto Torres
Alghero
Tavolara I.
C.Bon
Tunis
G. of Tunis
Biserta
Ras el Abiad
Galita I.
Bona
40
38
8
10
12
14
16
18
John Bartholomew & Co., Edinr.

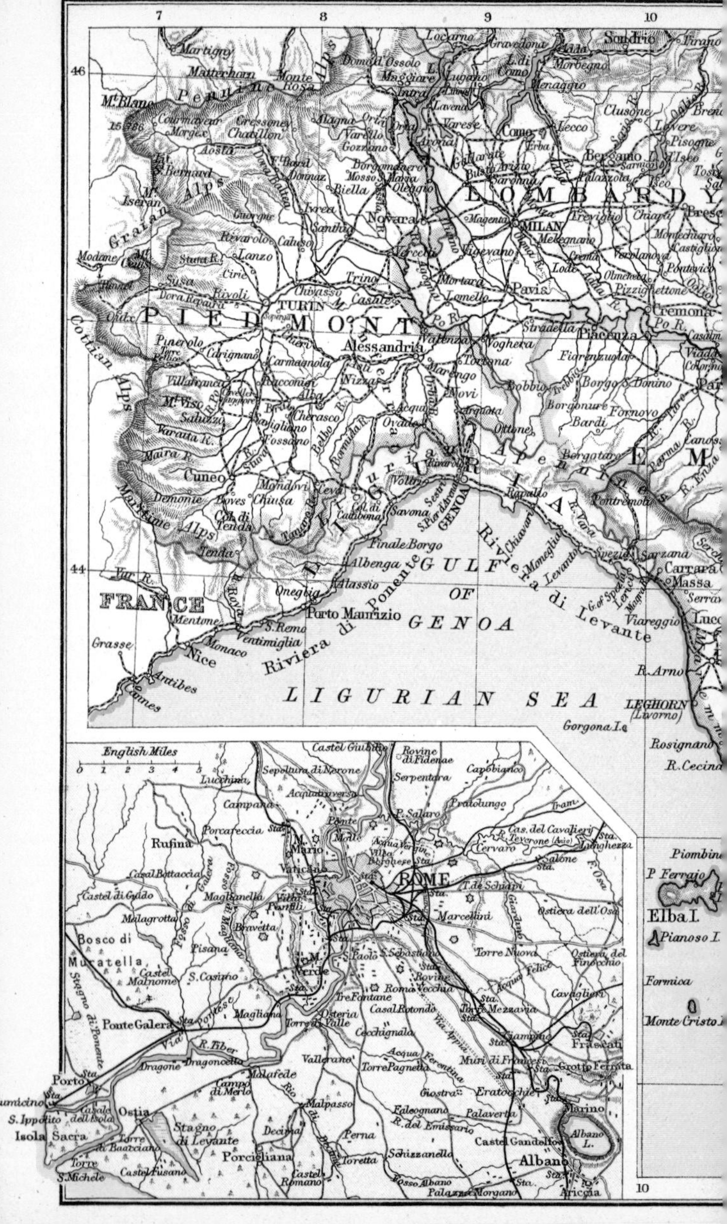

7
8
9
10
46
44
Locarno
Gravedona
Sondrio
Tirano
Martigny
Domod'Ossolo
L. Maggiore
Lugano
L. di Como
Morbegno
Menaggio
Matterhorn
Monte Rosa
Pennine
Alps
Mt. Blanc
15,786
Courmayeur
Morgex
Gressoney
Chatillon
Alagna
Orta
Varallo
Gozzano
Intra
Laveno
Varese
Arona
Como
Lecco
Clusone
Lovere
Pisogne
L. d'Iseo
Aosta
Bard
Donnaz
Borgomanero
Biella
Oleggio
Gallarate
Busto Arizio
Saronno
Erba
Bergamo
Palazzola
LOMBARDY
Brescia
Treviglio
Chiari
St. Bernard
Mt. Iseran
Graian Alps
Ivrea
Santhia
Novara
Magenta
MILAN
Melegnano
Montechiaro
Castiglione
Modane
Mt. Cenis
Caluso
Rivarolo
Lanzo
Stura R.
Cirie
Vercelli
Vigevano
Crema
Lodi
Pontevico
Olmeneta
Pizzighettone
Susa
Rivoli
Dora Riparia
Chivasso
Trino
Casale
Mortara
Lomello
Pavia
Cremona
Po R.
Oulx
PIEDMONT
TURIN
Superga
Chieri
Alessandria
Valenza
Voghera
Stradella
Piacenza
Cottian Alps
Pinerolo
Torre Pellice
Carignano
Carmagnola
Racconigi
Asti
Nizza
Tortona
Marengo
Novi
Fiorenzuola
Borgo S. Donino
Bobbio
Villafranca
Mt. Viso
Saluzzo
Bra
Alba
Cherasco
Savigliano
Fossano
Acqui
Ovada
Arquata
Ottone
Borgonure
Bardi
Fornovo
Varaita R.
Maira R.
Cuneo
Mondovi
Ceva
Chiusa
Boves
Demonte
Col di Tenda
Col di Cadibona
Tenda
Maritime Alps
LIGURIA
Apennine
Borgotaro
Pontremoli
Savona
Sestri
Voltri
GENOA
Rapallo
Chiavari
Moneglia
Levanto
Spezia
Sarzana
Carrara
Massa
Finale Borgo
Albenga
Alassio
Oneglia
Porto Maurizio
GULF OF GENOA
Riviera di Ponente
Riviera di Levante
Viareggio
Lucca
FRANCE
Var R.
Mentone
S. Remo
Ventimiglia
Monaco
Nice
Grasse
Antibes
Cannes
R. Arno
LIGURIAN SEA
LEGHORN (Livorno)
Gorgona I.
Rosignano
R. Cecina
English Miles
0 1 2 3 4 5
Castel Giubileo
Rovine di Fidenae
Sepoltura di Nerone
Serpentara
Capobianco
Lucchina
Acquatraversa
Campana
Pratolungo
P. Salaro
Ponte Molle
Porcareccia
M. Mario
Cas. del Cavalieri
R. Teverone (Anio)
Cervaro
Lunghezza
Rufina
Villa Borghese
Salone
Vaticano
ROME
Casal Bottaccia
T. de Schiavi
Castel di Guido
Magliana
Villa Panfili
Marcellina
Ostiera dell' Osa
Malagrotta
Bravetta
Bosco di Muratella
Pisana
S. Paolo
S. Sebastiano
Torre Nuova
Ostiera del Finocchio
Castel Malnome
S. Cosimo
M. Verde
Rovine
Roma Vecchia
Acqua Felice
Tre Fontane
Casal Rotondo
Cavaglieri
Ponte Galera
Magliana
Osteria Valle
Torre
Torre Mezzavia
Stagno di Ponente
R. Tiber
Via Portuense
Cecchignola
Via Appia
Ciampino
Frascati
Dragone
Dragoncello
Vallerano
Acqua Ferentina
Torre Pagnella
Muri di Francesi
Grotta Ferrata
Porto
Malafede
Campo di Merlo
Giostra
Fiumicino
Casale dell' Isola
Malpasso
Eratocchie
Marino
S. Ippolito
Isola Sacra
Ostia
Stagno di Levante
Torre di Boacciano
Decima
Perna
Falcognano
R. del Emissario
Palaverta
Albano L.
Castel Gandolfo
Porcigliana
Schizzanello
Toretta
Albano
Torre S. Michele
Castel Fusano
Castel Romano
Fosso Albano
Palazzo Morgano
Ariccia
Sta.
Piombino
P. Ferrajo
Elba I.
Pianosa I.
Formica
Monte Cristo

NORTHERN & CENTRAL
ITALY
English Miles
0
20
40
60
GULF OF VENICE
VENETIA
AUSTRIA-HUNGARY
Istria
MARCHES
UMBRIA
ROME
ABRUZZI AND MOLISE
Venice
Trieste
Ancona
Perugia
Florence
Rome
John Bartholomew & Co., Edin.

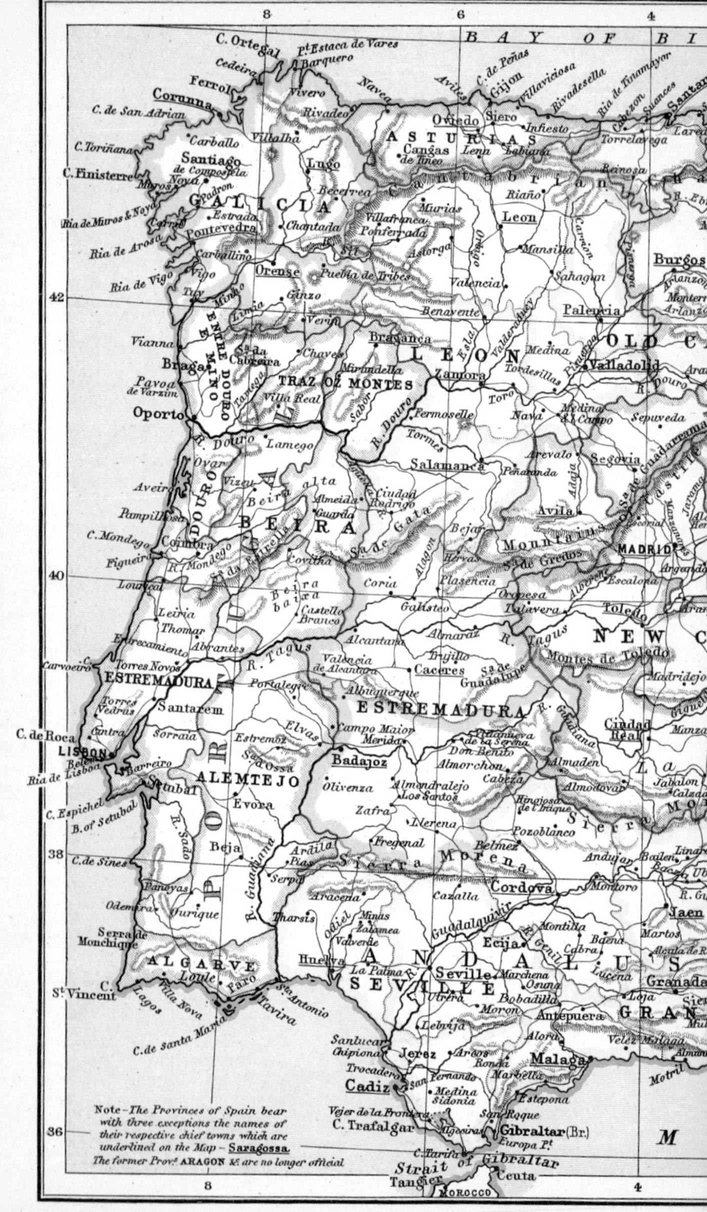
BAY OF BI
ASTURIAS
GALICIA
LEON
OLD C
BEIRA
TRAZ OZ MONTES
ENTRE DOURO E MINHO
ESTREMADURA
ALEMTEJO
ALGARVE
NEW C
ANDALUS
SEVILLE
GRAN
Corunna
Ferrol
Santiago de Compostela
Lugo
Oviedo
Gijon
Leon
Burgos
Palencia
Valladolid
Zamora
Salamanca
Avila
Segovia
MADRID
Toledo
Oporto
Braga
Coimbra
LISBON
Santarem
Evora
Beja
Faro
Caceres
Badajoz
Ciudad Real
Cordova
Seville
Huelva
Cadiz
Malaga
Granada
Jaen
Gibraltar (Br.)
Strait of Gibraltar
Tangier
Ceuta
MOROCCO
C. Finisterre
C. Ortegal
C. de Roca
C. St Vincent
C. Trafalgar
R. Douro
R. Tagus
R. Guadiana
Guadalquivir
Sierra Morena
Note – The Provinces of Spain bear with three exceptions the names of their respective chief towns which are underlined on the Map – Saragossa.
The former Provs. ARAGON &c. are no longer official

John Bartholomew & Co., Edinr.

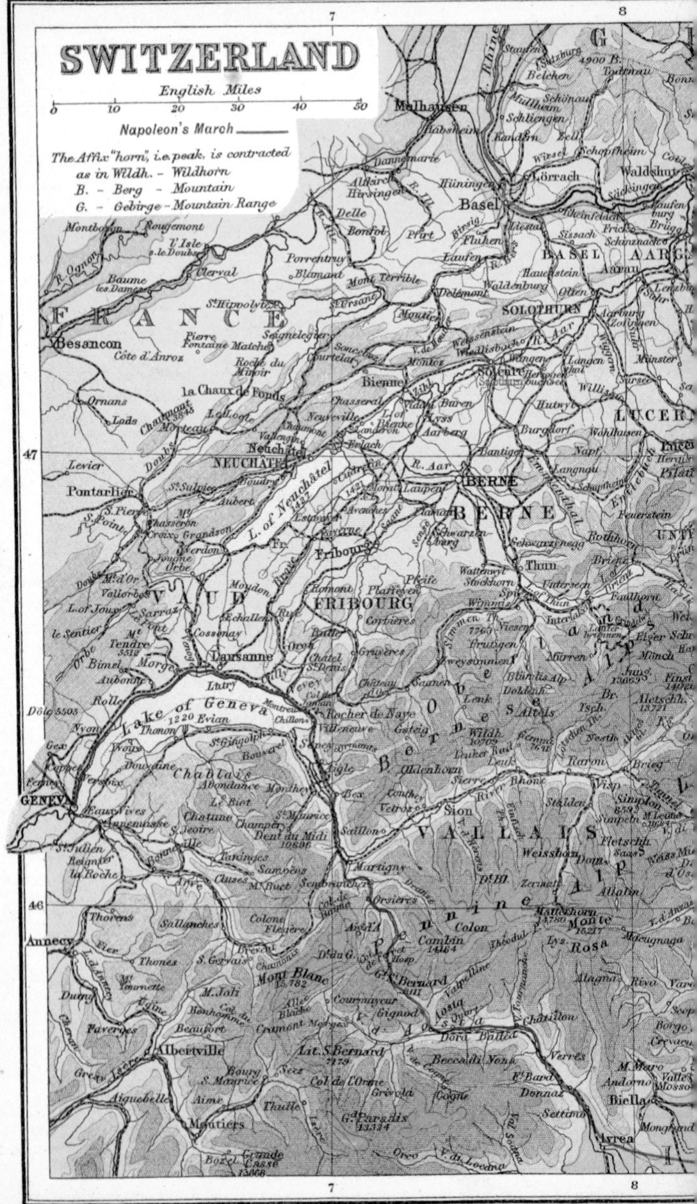
SWITZERLAND
English Miles
0 10 20 30 40 50
Napoleon's March
The Affix "horn", i.e. peak, is contracted
as in Wildh. - Wildhorn
B. - Berg - Mountain
G. - Gebirge - Mountain Range
F R A N C E
Besancon
Mulhausen
Basel
Lörrach
Waldshut
BASEL
SOLOTHURN
Solothurn
Delémont
Porrentruy
Mont Terrible
Bienne
La Chaux de Fonds
Neuchâtel
NEUCHÂTEL
L. of Neuchâtel
BERNE
B E R N E
Fribourg
FRIBOURG
V A U D
Lausanne
Lake of Geneva
GENEVA
Thun
Interlaken
Pontarlier
Yverdon
Vevey
Montreux
Villeneuve
Aigle
Sion
Martigny
V A L L A I S
Simplon
Matterhorn
Monte Rosa
Mont Blanc
Gd. S. Bernard
Aosta
Lit. S. Bernard
Albertville
Annecy
Chamonix
Moutiers
Ivrea
Biella
Jung.
Eiger
Mönch
Lucerne
Aarau
Burgdorf
Chablais
Dent du Midi
Bernese Alps
Pennine Alps
River Rhone
R. Aar
Thonon
Evian
Nyon
Rolle
Morges
Orbe
Doubs
Levier
Ornans
Baume les Dames
Clerval
Rougemont
Montbozon
Sallanches
Bonneville
St. Julien
Chatillon
Verres
Gd. Paradis
Grande Casse
46
47
7
8

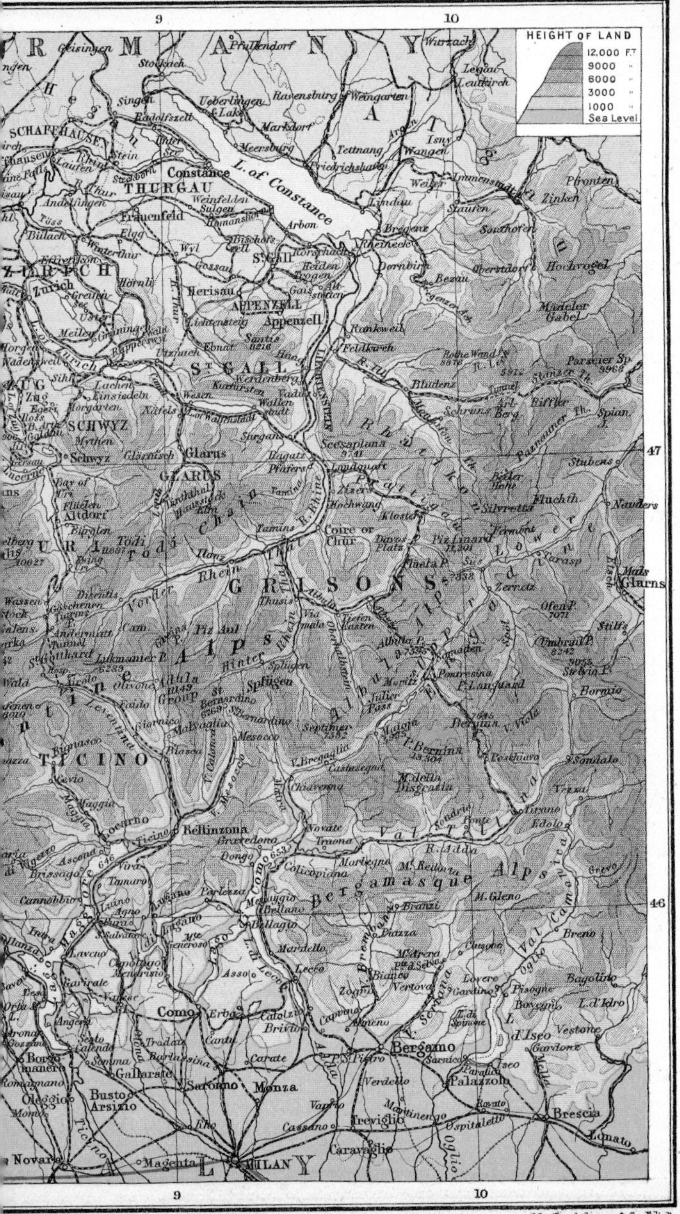
HEIGHT OF LAND
12,000 F.T
9000
6000
3000
1000
Sea Level
L. of Constance
Constance
THURGAU
Zurich
St Gall
APPENZELL
Appenzell
SCHWYZ
Schwyz
Glarus
GLARUS
Altdorf
GRISONS
Coire or Chur
TICINO
Bellinzona
Locarno
Como
Lecco
Bergamo
Brescia
MILAN
Monza
Bergamasque Alps
Val Tellina
9
10
47
46

(SCANDINAVIA)

SWEDEN, NORWAY & DENMARK.

English Miles 0 50 100 150 200

SWEDEN. Læns or Districts.	NORWAY. Amts or Bailliewicks.
1 Norrbotten	1 Finmarken I[a]. Tromsö
2 Westerbotten	2 Nordland
3 Jemtland	3 North Trondhjem
4 Wester Norrbotten	4 Romsdal
5 Gefleborg	5 South Drontheim
6 Kopparberg	6 Hedemarken
7 Wermland	7 Christians
8 Örebro	8 North Bergenhuus
9 Westmanland	9 South Bergenhuus
10 Upsala	10 Stavanger
11 Stockholm	11 Lister & Mandal
Stockholm (town)	12 Nedenaes & Robygdel
12 Södermanland	13 Bratsberg
13 Öster Gothland	14 Buskerud
14 Skaraborg	15 Jarlsberg
15 Elfsborg	16 Agershuus
16 Götheborg & Bohus	Christiania (town)
17 Halland	17 Smaalenen
18 Jönköping	
19 Calmar	
20 Kronoberg	
21 Blekinge	
22 Christianstad	
23 Malmöhus	
24 Gothland	

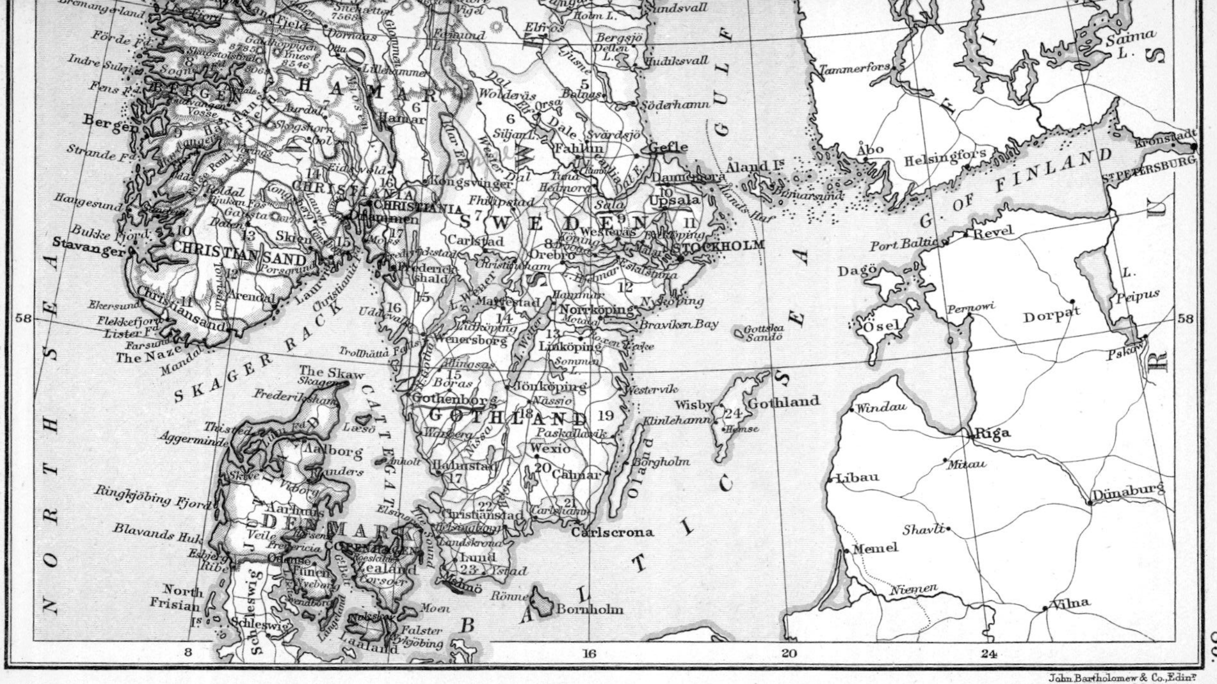

NORTH SEA
SKAGER RACK
CATTEGAT
GULF OF FINLAND
BALTIC SEA
SWEDEN
DENMARK
GOTHLAND
FINLAND
RUSSIA
HAMAR
BERGEN
CHRISTIANIA
CHRISTIANSAND
STOCKHOLM
St. PETERSBURG
Kronstadt
Saima L.
Tammerfors
Åbo
Helsingfors
Åland Is.
Bomarsund
Ålands Haf
Revel
Port Baltic
Dagö
Ösel
Pernowi
Dorpat
L. Peipus
Pskow
Windau
Riga
Mitau
Libau
Dünaburg
Shavli
Memel
Niemen
Vilna
Gotska Sandö
Wisby
Gothland
Klintehamn
Hemse
Bornholm
Rönne
Carlscrona
Öland
Borgholm
Calmar
Wexio
Paskallavik
Westervik
Jönköping
Nässjö
Linköping
Norrköping
Motala
Braviken Bay
Nyköping
Eskilstuna
Westerås
Köping
Upsala
Dannemora
Gefle
Söderhamn
Hudiksvall
Bergsjö
Ljusne
Balnäs
Fahlun
Dale
Orsa
Siljan L.
Wolderäs
Wester Dal
Klar Elf
Kongsvinger
Philipstad
Carlstad
Christinehamn
Örebro
L. Hjelmar
L. Wener
L. Wetter
Mariestad
Lidköping
Wenersborg
Trollhätta Falls
Uddevalla
Frederickshald
Moss
Drammen
Christiania
Eidsvold
Hamar
Lillehammer
Fjeld
Dovre Fjeld
Skien
Arendal
Christiansand
Flekkefjord
Lister Fd.
Farsund
Mandal
The Naze
Ekersund
Stavanger
Bulkke Fjord
Haugesund
Strande Fd.
Bergen
Fens Fd.
Indre Sulen
Förde Fd.
Bremangerland
Vosse
Gol
Kongsberg
Lauven
Porsgrund
Laurvig
Christiania Fd.
Torrisdal
Gothenborg
Borås
Alingsås
Warberg
Halmstad
Nissa
Christianstad
Carlshamn
Landskrona
Lund
Ystad
Malmö
Elsinore
The Sound
Anholt
Læsö
The Skaw
Skagen
Frederikshavn
Aalborg
Randers
Viborg
Aarhus
Thisted
Aggermunde
Ringkjöbing Fjord
Blavands Huk
Esbjerg
Ribe
Veile
Horsens
Fredericia
Odense
Fünen
Nyborg
Svendborg
G.t Belt
Langeland
Copenhagen
Roeskilde
Zealand
Corsoer
Moen
Falster
Nykjöbing
Laaland
Nakskov
Schleswig
North Frisian Is.
58
8
16
20
24
John Bartholomew & Co., Edinr.

RUSSIA IN EUROPE

English Miles 0 100 200 300

North Cape
Novaia Zemlia
Kara Sea
Waigatz
Kolguev
Kola Peninsula
WHITE SEA
LAPLAND
SWEDEN
FINLAND
Gulf of Bothnia
G. of Finland
BALTIC SEA
ARCHANGEL
OLONETZ
VOLOGDA
NOVGOROD
PSKOV
TVER
YAROSLAV
KOSTROMA
VIATKA
PERM
ESTHONIA
LIVONIA
COURLAND
KOVNO
VITEBSK
RUSSIA
SIBERIA
Ural Mountains
Gulf of Obi
R. Ob or Obi
Samoieds
Arctic Circle
ST PETERSBURG
STOCKHOLM
Archangel
Mezen
Onega
Vologda
Novgorod
Kostroma
Yaroslavl
Nijni Novgorod
Kazan
Viatka
Perm
Ekaterinburg
Riga
Reval
Königsberg
Helsingfors
Åland Is.
Lake Ladoga
L. Onega
L. Peipus
Ilmen L.
Bielo-sero L.
Kubinskoie L.

POLAND
Warsaw
Cracow
GRODNO
MINSK
MOHILEV
KALUGA
TULA
RIASAN
PENZA
SIMBIRSK
SAMARA
Samara
ORENBURG
Orenburg
TAMBOV
OREL
KURSK
VORONESH
SARATOV
Saratov
TCHERNIGOV
VOLHYNIA
KIEV
Kiev
PODOLIA
POLTAVA
KHARKOV
Kharkov
EKATERINOSLAV
KHERSON
BESSARABIA
Odessa
SOUTH RUSSIA
DON COSSACKS
ASTRAKHAN
Astrakhan
Kirghiz Horde
(to Orenburg)
Mouths of the Volga
URALSK
Orenburg Khirghiz
Ust-Urt Plateau
TRANSCASPIAN TERRITORY
CASPIAN SEA
Sea of Azov
Crimea
Sevastopol
STAVROPOL
Stavropol
Kuban Dist.
Terek Dist.
DAGHESTAN
CAUCASUS
Tiflis
BAKU
Baku
ERIVAN
Krasnovodsk
AUSTRIA HUNGARY
Lemberg
ROUMANIA
Bukharest
BULGARIA
EAST ROUMELIA
TURKEY
CONSTANTINOPLE
Sea of Marmora
ÆGEAN SEA
BLACK SEA
Sinope
Trebizond
Erzerum
Angora
ASIA MINOR
R. Volga
R. Don
R. Ural
Dnieper
Dniester
R. Danube
John Bartholomew & Co., Edinr.

KINGDOM OF POLAND
Kingdom of Poland before union with Lithuania
" " at greatest extent
Poland in the time of Napoleon I
Present Limits of Russia, Prussia and Austria
BALTIC SEA
PRUSSIA
LITHUANIA
RUSSIA
POLAND
Silesia
Galicia
Carpathian Mts
AUSTRIA-HUNGARY
SOUTH RUSSIA
Ukraine
Volhynia
Podolia
Courland
Livonia
Esthonia
Cossacks of the Don
Gulf of Riga
Rokitno Swamps
MOSCOW
Warsaw
Cracow
Vilna
Kovno
Grodno
Minsk
Kiev
Smolensk
Vitebsk
Mohilev
Riga
Dünaburg
Pskov
Novgorod
Tver
Kaluga
Tula
Riazan
Orel
Kursk
Kharkov
Poltava
Voronesh
Tambov
Penza
Saratov
Simbirsk
Ekaterinoslav
Königsberg
Danzig
Stettin
Berlin
Breslau
Prague
Brünn
Vienna
Buda Pest
Lublin
Radom
Kielce
Lodz
Kalisz
Plotsk
Lomza
Suvalki
Bielostok
Brest-Litovsk
Pinsk
Siedlce
Lemberg
Kamenetz Podolsk
Berdichev
Shitomir
Chernigov
English Miles
0 100 200

John Bartholomew & Co., Edinr.

AUSTRIA-HUNGARY
TRANSYLVANIA
BESSARABIA
MOLDAVIA
ROUMANIA
WALLACHIA
BULGARIA
EASTERN ROUMELIA
SERVIA
BOSNIA
HERZEGOVINA
MONTENEGRO
DALMATIA
SLAVONIA
BANAT
BLACK SEA
ADRIATIC
Carpathians
Transylvanian Alps
Balkan Mts.
Dinaric Alps
BUDA PEST
BUKHAREST
BELGRADE
SOFIA
CETIGNE
River Danube
R. Pruth
R. Sereth
R. Dniester
R. Maros
R. Szamos
R. Theiss
R. Drave or Drau
R. Save or Sau
R. Drina
R. Morava
R. Timok
R. Isker
R. Aluta
R. Arjish
R. Jalomitza
R. Ibar
R. Lim
L. Balaton
Agram
Essek
Nagy Kanissa
Debreczin
Grosswardein
Klausenburg
Hermanstadt
Kronstadt
Maros Vasarhely
Szegedin
Temesvar
Maria Theresiopel
Zombor
Neusatz
Semlin
Pancsova
Bazias
Kishenev
Bendery
Ismail
Kilia
Jassy
Roman
Botoshani
Galatz
Braila
Fokshany
Rimnik
Ploesti
Pitesti
Krajova
Turnu Severin
Kalafat
Widin
Lom Palanka
Rahova
Nicopoli
Sistova
Rustchuk
Silistria
Tirnova
Plevna
Shumla
Varna
Kustendji
Burghas
Philippopolis
Adrianople
Kostendil
Nish
Pirot
Alexinatz
Kragujevatz
Semendria
Novibazar
Seraievo
Mostar
Cattaro
Ragusa
Spalato
Skutari
Prisrend

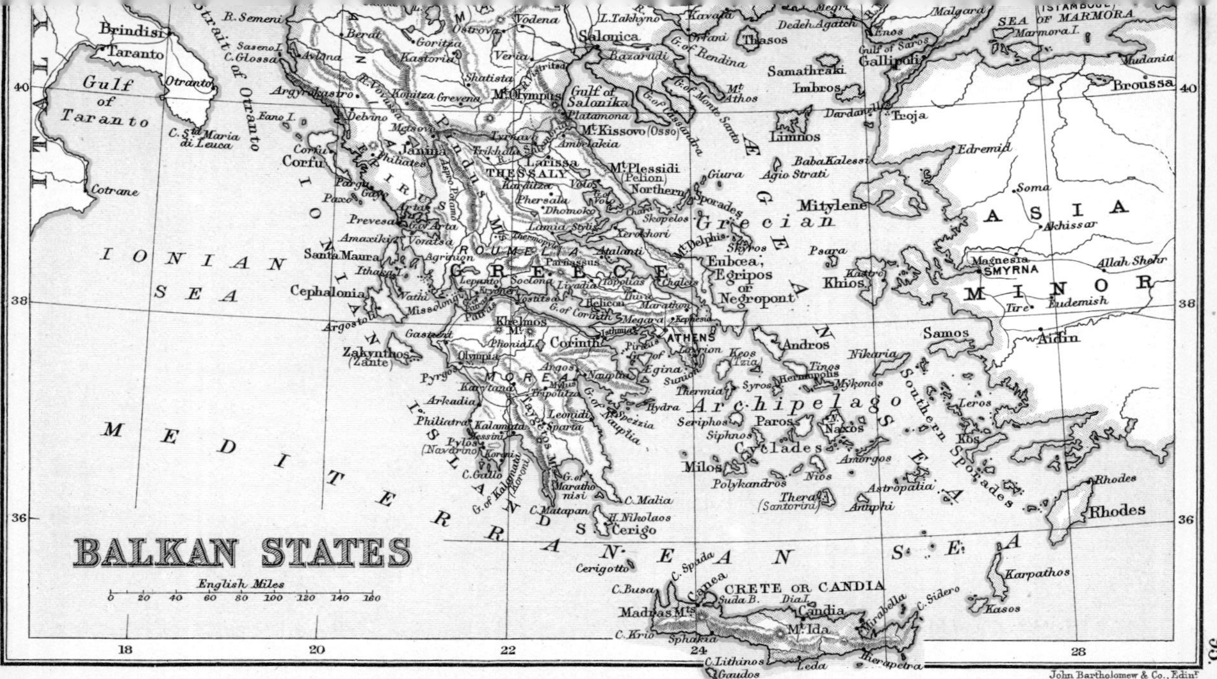
BALKAN STATES
English Miles
0 20 40 60 80 100 120 140 160
John Bartholomew & Co., Edinr
ASIA MINOR
SEA OF MARMORA
Broussa
SMYRNA
Aidin
Samos
Rhodes
Karpathos
Kasos
Southern Sporades
Archipelago
Cyclades
Naxos
Paros
Andros
Tinos
Mykonos
Milos
Thera (Santorini)
CRETE OR CANDIA
Candia
Mt. Ida
Gaudos
Cerigo
ATHENS
Corinth
Eubœa, Egripos or Negropont
Khios
Mitylene
Grecian
Limnos
Imbros
Samothraki
Thasos
Gallipoli
Troja
Salonica
Larissa
THESSALY
Pindus Mts.
Epirus
Janina
Corfu
Santa Maura
Cephalonia
Zakynthos (Zante)
IONIAN SEA
MEDITERRANEAN SEA
Morea
Taygetos Mts.
Strait of Otranto
Gulf of Taranto
Brindisi
Taranto
Otranto

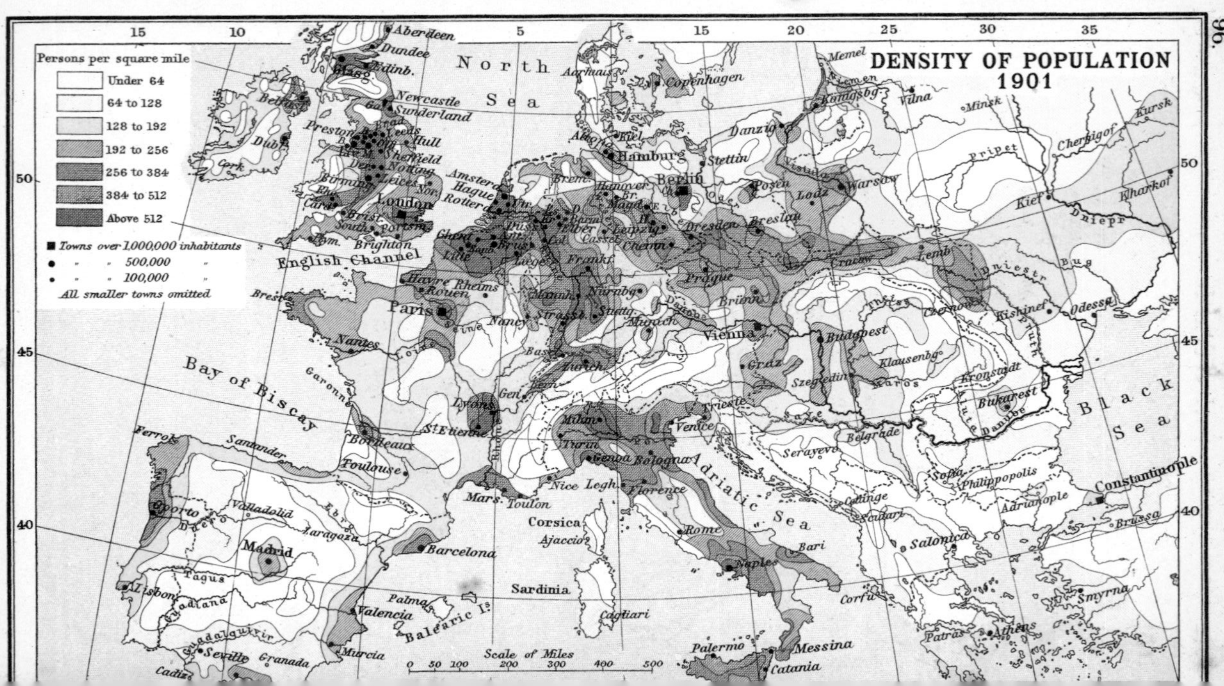
DENSITY OF POPULATION
1901
Persons per square mile
Under 64
64 to 128
128 to 192
192 to 256
256 to 384
384 to 512
Above 512
Towns over 1,000,000 inhabitants
" " 500,000 "
" " 100,000 "
All smaller towns omitted
Scale of Miles
0 50 100 200 300 400 500
North Sea
English Channel
Bay of Biscay
Adriatic Sea
Black Sea
Aberdeen
Dundee
Edinb.
Glasg.
Newcastle
Sunderland
Preston
Hull
Belfast
Dubl.
Cork
London
Brighton
Bristol
Birmingham
Nottingham
Sheffield
Amsterd.
Hague
Rotterd.
Aarhaus
Copenhagen
Memel
Niemen
Konigsbg.
Vilna
Minsk
Kursk
Chernigof
Pripet
Kief
Kharkof
Dniepr
Danzig
Kiel
Altona
Hamburg
Stettin
Berlin
Brem.
Hanover
Magd.
Posen
Warsaw
Lodz
Vistula
Dresden
Breslau
Leipzig
Cassel
Chemn.
Ghent
Lille
Liege
Col.
Frankf.
Cracow
Lemb.
Dniestr
Bug
Odessa
Kishinef
Pruth
Prague
Brünn
Havre
Rheims
Rouen
Paris
Brest
Mannh.
Nurnbg.
Stuttg.
Munich
Strassb.
Nancy
Seine
Loire
Nantes
Danube
Vienna
Budapest
Theiss
Chernowitz
Klausenbg.
Maros
Kronstadt
Bukarest
Aluta
Graz
Szegedin
Basel
Zurich
Bern
Gen.
Garonne
Lyons
St.Etienne
Rhone
Bordeaux
Toulouse
Milan
Turin
Venice
Trieste
Save
Belgrade
Serayevo
Genoa
Bologna
Nice
Legh.
Florence
Mars.
Toulon
Cettinge
Scutari
Sofia
Philippopolis
Adrianople
Constantinople
Brussa
Ferrol
Santander
Oporto
Duero
Valladolid
Ebro
Zaragoza
Madrid
Tagus
Lisbon
Guadiana
Guadalquivir
Seville
Granada
Cadiz
Barcelona
Valencia
Murcia
Palma
Balearic Is.
Corsica
Ajaccio
Sardinia
Cagliari
Rome
Naples
Bari
Palermo
Messina
Catania
Corfu
Salonica
Patras
Athens
Smyrna

A BRIEF SURVEY OF THE ENGLISH COINAGE FROM THE EARLIEST TIMES TO THE PRESENT DAY

PLATE I.

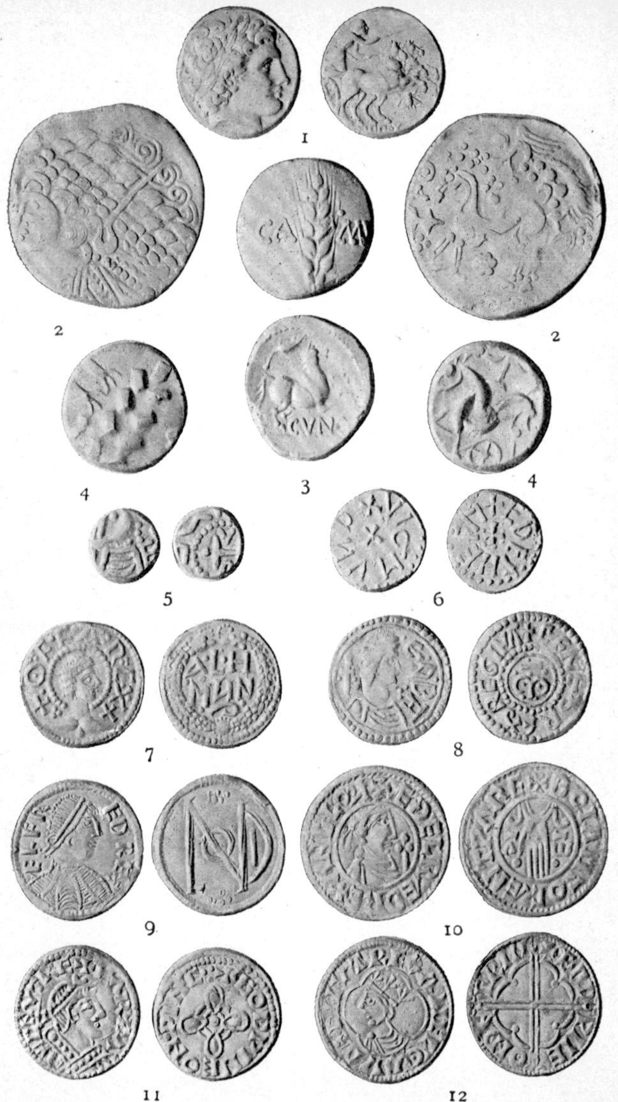

A BRIEF SURVEY
OF THE
ENGLISH COINAGE
FROM THE EARLIEST TIMES TO THE PRESENT DAY

By BERNARD ROTH, F.S.A.

Vice-President of British Numismatic Society and Member of Council of Royal Numismatic Society.

THE ancient Britons were intimately related to their neighbours the Gauls on the other side of the English Channel, and through them early obtained a knowledge of a well-designed coinage, chiefly of gold, which was minted for nearly 250 years. According to Sir John Evans, the gold uninscribed coins of the south coast were probably first issued between 200 and 150 B.C. These gold coins are usually described as staters, because they are degenerate copies of the beautifully executed gold staters of Philip II., King of Macedon, father of Alexander the Great (B.C. 382-336).

Fig. I., Plate I., is a gold stater of that king; on the *obverse, i.e.*, the more important side, of the coin, which usually carries the king's head or the chief symbol, is a laureate head of Apollo or Hercules looking to the right; on the other side (*reverse*) is a charioteer in a biga, or two-horsed chariot, with two wheels.

Fig. II., Plate I., is an ancient British gold coin of about B.C. 150, which is a barbarous copy of the perfect Greek art seen in Fig. I. On the obverse is a large head to the left with extremely ornate hair, etc., while on the reverse is a very disjointed horse with the remnants of a winged charioteer.

Fig. III., Plate I., is a fine specimen of a later ancient British inscribed coin of Cunobelinus (Shakespeare's Cymbeline), a British king who flourished about A.D. 5: his capital was Camulodonum, on the site of which is modern Colchester. On the obverse is a horse with CVNO below, and on the reverse is an ear of wheat with CA MV on either side. The latest and most barbarously designed ancient British coins were those of the Brigantes, a tribe who inhabited Yorkshire, Lancashire, and other northern counties. Some years before their conquest by the Romans in A.D. 69, their queen was Cartismandua, who is said to have treacherously delivered up to the invaders Caractacus who had taken refuge in her court.

Fig. IV., Plate I., is a gold stater of the Brigantes, in which it is still possible to find some distant resemblance to the design on Philip's coin. On the obverse there are remains of the wreath with locks of hair, but it is difficult to picture any likeness to a face. These ancient Britons were far more civilised than many historians have described them to be. I have several contemporary forgeries of ancient British staters in my collection. They consist of copper covered with a thin plating of gold: a high degree of mechanical skill was required to produce such a forged coin.

For several centuries after the Roman invasion all traces of a native coinage disappear till we come to the period of the Sceats and Stycas. The sceats were the earliest Saxon coins struck in England, and were chiefly in silver, although gold specimens are known.

Fig. V., Plate I., is a gold sceat which is supposed to have been struck by Abbo, a Frankish moneyer who accompanied St. Augustine to England in A.D. 596: on the obverse is a rude bust to the left with E behind; on the reverse traces of letters around a dotted inner border enclosing a large H-shaped ornament in centre, with letters above and below. The stycas resemble the sceats, but are usually of very base silver or copper.

Fig. VI., Plate I., is a copper styca of Vigmund, Archbishop of York (A.D. 837-854). The silver penny or, as it was called in early days, the *novus denarius* was of Frankish origin, and was first struck by Pepin the Short in 755. This coin rapidly became popular all over Europe, and drove out, not only the up to then current Roman coins, but also the sceats and the stycas. Offa, King of Mercia (A.D. 757-796), was the first English prince to strike silver pennies, and all his coins are of beautiful types.

Fig. VII., Plate I., is a silver penny of King Offa, while Fig. VIII., Plate I., is one of his widowed queen, Cynethryth, who reigned for one year after his death. Contrary to the almost universal custom, the queen's name is on the reverse of the coin, while the name of the mint master, or moneyer, EOBA, is on the obverse, in front of the queen's bust. For many centuries the silver penny was the only current English coin, and when smaller change was required it was cut into halves and quarters to form halfpennies and farthings, an operation which was often helped by the large cross on the reverse.

Fig. IX., Plate I., is a penny of Alfred the Great (871-901), with the monogram of London on the reverse: the portrait of the king on the obverse is fairly good, but the whole coin is far inferior in execution to those of King Offa and his queen. Aethelred II. (979-1016) struck a large number of different types; one of the most interesting of his pennies is shown in Fig. X., Plate I., with the king's head on the obverse and the so-called hand of Providence between A and ω descending from the clouds on the reverse. Our Danish King Canute (1016-1035) issued a number of different pennies, of which Fig. XI., Plate I., is one which was minted at Dover. Fig. XII., Plate I., is a penny of Harold I. (1035-1040), and Fig. XIII., Plate II., a penny of Harthacnut (1040-1042). Silver pennies of Edward the Confessor (1042-1066) were struck in upwards of sixty different English towns, and are of various types. Fig. XIV., Plate II., represents his "sovereign" type. On the obverse the king is seen sitting on his throne, holding the sceptre in the right hand and the orb in the left; on the reverse we have what is termed a short cross voided with a martlet (bird) in each of the four quarters: this has usually been described as the Confessor's arms. Harold II. (1066), although he reigned only a few months, struck some coins of which Fig. XV., Plate II., represents a penny, with the king's head to the left with the sceptre in front; on the reverse we find PAX (Peace) across the coin, which is rather incongruous, seeing he met his death so soon after at the Battle of Hastings. William the Conqueror (1066-1087) struck pennies with a good portrait of himself, of which Fig. XVI., Plate II., is a fine specimen: it is usually termed the bonnet type, owing to the curious head-dress or crown

PLATE II.

13 14 15 16 17 18 19 20 21 22 24 23 24

on the king's head. William Rufus (1087-1100) did not vary much the coins of his father, and Fig. XVII., Plate II., represents a penny of his struck at Ipswich.

Henry I. (1100-1135) struck several types, of which Fig. XVIII., Plate II., minted at London, is an interesting specimen. Stephen's troubled reign (1135-1154) is reflected by the clumsy and badly struck pennies of his coinage. One rarely ever meets with a well struck and round coin of this king. Fig. XIX., Plate II., is a Stephen penny struck at Gloucester. The Empress Matilda, daughter of Henry I., was Queen of England for a year during this reign, and struck coins in several towns.

Fig. XX., Plate II., represents what is considered a fine specimen of a Matilda penny. In spite of the bad execution of the coins of Stephen and Matilda, the silver employed was not debased. Henry II. (1154-1189), after his first issue, struck the "short cross" penny, of which Fig. XXI., Plate II., is a specimen minted at Worcester. This same "short cross" penny was struck without alteration of type and with the same name, Henricus, during the succeeding reigns of Richard I. (1189-1199) and John (1199-1216), and was continued unchanged during the greater portion of the reign of Henry III. (1216-1272), till the year 1248, when the "long cross" penny was struck: in this, the voided or double-lined cross on the reverse extends to the margin of the coin instead of only to the inner circle, as in the short cross variety. This king also added the numerals III. (or the Latin equivalent) after his name, to distinguish himself from his predecessors, the first time this device was employed in the English coinage (*see* Fig. XXII., Plate II., which is a long cross penny of Henry III.).

Edward I. (1272-1307) coined for the first time halfpennies and farthings, instead of having pennies cut into halves and quarters, as had been the custom till that time. Fig. XXIII., Plate II., is a farthing struck at York. The coinage of Edward II. (1307-1327) is so similar to that of Edward I. that even experts differ amongst themselves as to whom they should be assigned. Edward III. (1327-1377) made several important innovations: he not only issued a gold coinage, but also larger silver coins, viz., groats (fourpence) and half groats (twopence); his second gold coinage was the Noble, shown in Fig. XXIV., Plate II. This beautiful

25

26

27

28

work of art was current for six shillings and eightpence. On the obverse the king standing in the ship, is supposed to refer to the victory over the French fleet off Sluys in 1340. Fig. XXV., Plate III., is a groat of Edward III. During this king's reign there was a great expansion of the Norman possessions of the English crown, with a corresponding increase in the output of Anglo-Gallic coins. Fig. XXVI., Plate III., is a gold Pavillon or Royal d'Or of his son, Edward the Black Prince. It is interesting to note that there are four ostrich feathers on the obverse of the coin, two on each side of the bust of that prince.

Richard II. (1377-1399) and Henry IV. (1399-1413), Henry V. (1413-1422) and Henry VI. (1422-1461), made little changes in the coinages, except that the last king struck two new coins, the angel and half angel. Fig. XXVII., Plate III., is the angel, which was current for six shillings and eightpence. On the obverse is the Archangel St. Michael piercing the dragon, and on the reverse a ship to the right with the mast shaped like a cross, surmounted by a top castle.

Edward IV. (1461-1483) issued one new coin, the rose noble, shown in Fig. XXVIII., Plate III., which differs from the noble by having the rose on the side of the ship and in the centre of the reverse. Rose nobles were not only struck at the Tower, but also at Bristol, Coventry, York (Eboracum), and Norwich, and to distinguish these several mints the initial letter of the town was placed on the waves below the ship: thus in the rose noble figured there is a B for Bristol. The coins of Edward V. (1483) were exactly like his father's, and are only to be distinguished by their mint marks. Richard III. (1483-1485) had no distinguishing coins.

Henry VII. (1485-1509) struck a very fine new gold coin, the sovereign, double the weight of the noble, viz., 240 grains, and was current for twenty shillings: it is shown in Fig. XXIX., Plate IV. This same king also issued the first shilling or testoon. Henry VIII. (1509-1547) struck two new gold coins, the gold crown and the gold George noble, which were current for five shillings, and six shillings and eightpence respectively. Fig. XXX., Plate IV., is the crown and Fig. XXXI., Plate IV., the George noble, which has on the reverse St. George in armour on horseback and

PLATE IV.

29

30 30

31 32 31

33

34 34

35 35

37

36 36

piercing the dragon. The shilling or testoon (Fig. XXXII., Plate IV.) gives a good portrait of the king.

Edward VI. (1547-1553) struck the first silver crown, shown in Fig. XXXIII., Plate IV. Mary (1553-1558), after her marriage with Philip II. of Spain, struck coins with the portrait of her husband as well as of herself, as seen in the shilling (Fig. XXXIV., Plate V.). The Spanish king's name is invariably placed first, before that of the English queen.

Elizabeth (1558-1603) issued a dated sixpence yearly for upwards of forty years, and Fig. XXXV., Plate V., is a milled sixpence of the year 1562: her dress is very ornate, as is the rule on all her coins.

When James VI. of Scotland became James I. of England (1603-1625) he struck several coins to symbolise the union of the kingdoms. Fig. XXXVI., Plate V., is the gold unite or sovereign. The reverse legend—"Faciam eos in gentem unam"—is from Ezekiel xxxvii. 22, "*I will make them one nation* in the land upon the mountains of Israel; and one king shall be king to them all: and they shall be no more two nations, neither shall they be divided into two kingdoms any more."

Charles I.'s troubled and tragic reign (1625-1649) produced innumerable new coins. While at Oxford, the gold three-pound piece (Fig. XXXVII., Plate V.) and the silver pound or twenty shilling piece (Fig. XXXVIII., Plate VI.) were made out of the melted-down plate of the Oxford colleges. Amongst the many siege pieces of this reign, the shilling of Pontefract Castle (Fig. XXXIX., Plate VI.) is very typical.

The Commonwealth coinage (1649-1660) is remarkable in having all the legends in good honest English instead of in Latin, and Fig. XL., Plate VI., represents the gold broad or twenty-shilling piece. Oliver Cromwell (1653-1658) had some coins struck with his portrait, but it is doubtful whether they were ever in circulation. The crown, by Thomas Simon (Fig. XLI., Plate VII.), is a fine work of art.

Charles II. (1660-1685) gave us the first five guinea piece (Fig. XLII., Plate VII.). His example was followed by James II. (1685-1688), William and Mary (1688-1694) (*see* Fig. XLIII., Plate VII.), William (1694-1702), Anne (1702-1714), and the first two Georges (1714-1760).

George III. (1760-1820) was the last king to issue the

1648
RELIG PROT
LEG ANG
LIBER PAR
1644
THE COMMONWEALTH OF ENGLAND
1649
GOD WITH VS

39 39

38

40

OLIVAR·D·G·R·P·ANG·SCO·HIB·&·PRO·
PAX·QVÆRITVR·BELLO 1658
·CAROLVS·II· DEI·GRATIA
1669·MAG·BR·FRA·ET·HIB·REX·
GVLIELMVS·ET·MARIA·DEI·GRATIA
1692·MAG·BR·FR·ET·HIB·REX·ET·REGINA·

41

42

43

1820
VICTORIA REGINA
ONE FLORIN
ONE TENTH OF A POUND
EDWARDVS VII DEI GRA: BRITT: OMN: REX FID: DEF: IND: IMP:
1902

44

45

46

47

guinea, of which the spade variety (Fig. XLIV., Plate VIII.) is well known. The modern sovereign of twenty shillings was first struck by this king (Fig. XLV., Plate VIII.).

The coinages of George IV. (1820-1830) and William IV. (1830-1837) have no new features.

Queen Victoria (1837-1902) issued two new silver coins, the double florin of four shillings and the florin of two shillings. The first florin (Fig. XLVI., Plate VIII.) was issued in 1849, and as the words "Dei Gratia" were omitted, it is known as the "godless or graceless florin."

Edward VII. (1902-1910) issued the same coins as his mother, from the five-pound piece down to the farthing, with the exception of the double florin. Fig. XLVII., Plate VIII., is his five-pound piece.

All the illustrations are from photographs of casts taken from coins in the author's collection.

MAPS AND PLANS

OF

NOTABLE BATTLES AND DISTRICTS

CONNECTED WITH

FAMOUS AUTHORS AND THEIR BOOKS

PLANS OF CLASSICAL AND OTHER BATTLES DESCRIBED BY CREASY IN "FIFTEEN DECISIVE BATTLES OF THE WORLD"

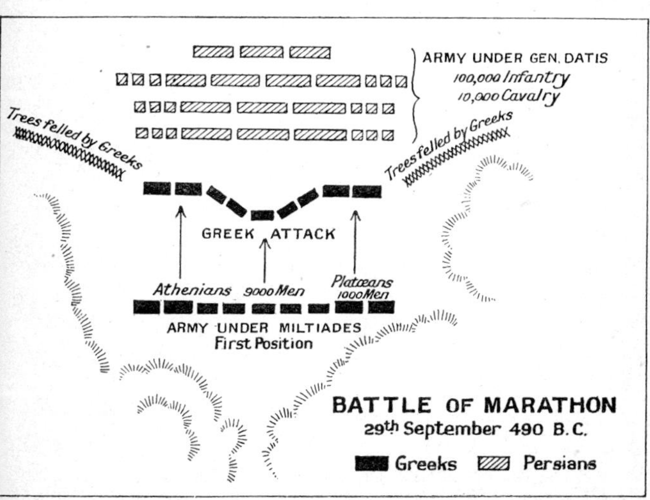

See Grote's "History of Greece." Creasy's "Fifteen Decisive Battles of the World." Rawlinson's "Herodotus," etc., etc.

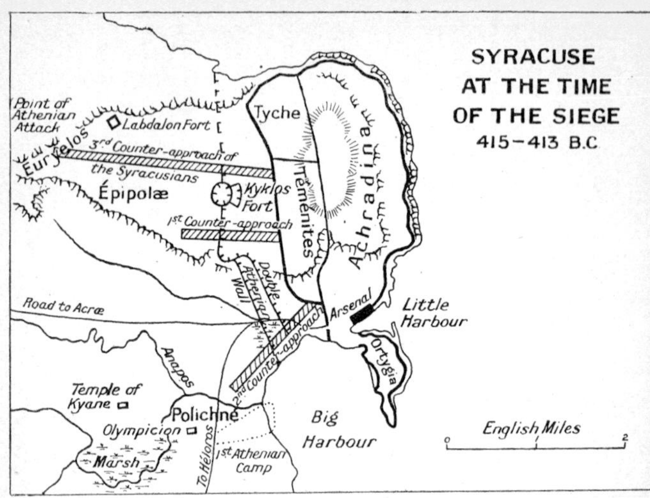

See Grote's "History of Greece." Creasy's "Fifteen Decisive Battles of the World," etc., etc.

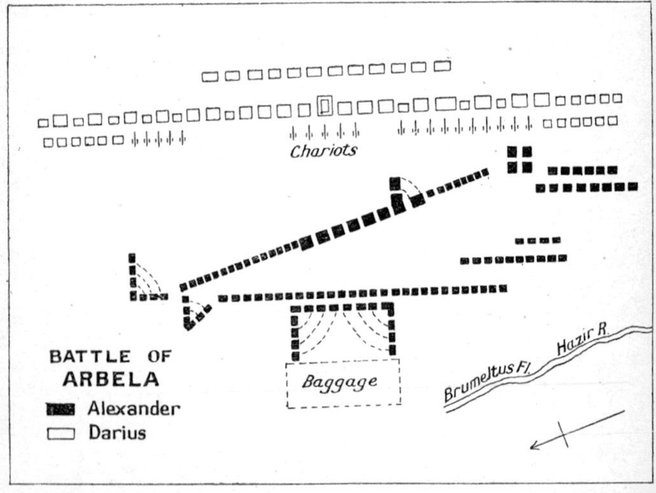

See Grote's "History of Greece." Creasy's "Fifteen Decisive Battles of the World," etc., etc.

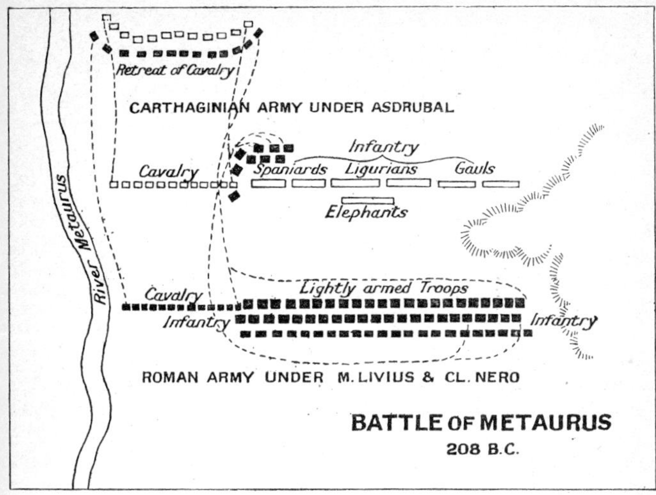

See Grote's "History of Greece." Creasy's "Fifteen Decisive Battles of the World," etc., etc.

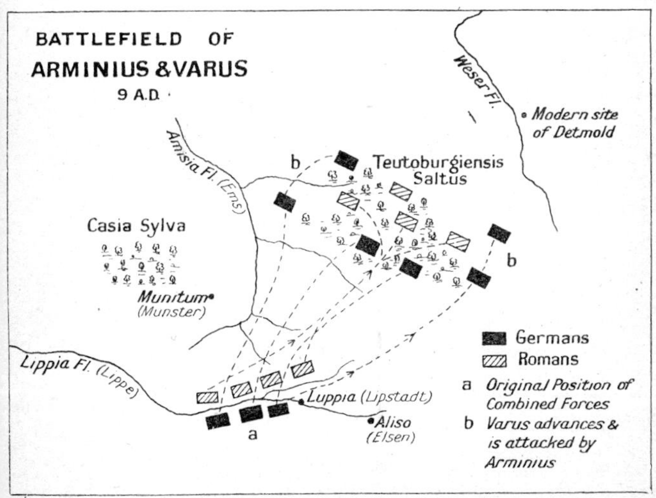

See Tacitus' "Agricola" and "Germania." Creasy's "Fifteen Decisive Battles of the World," etc., etc.

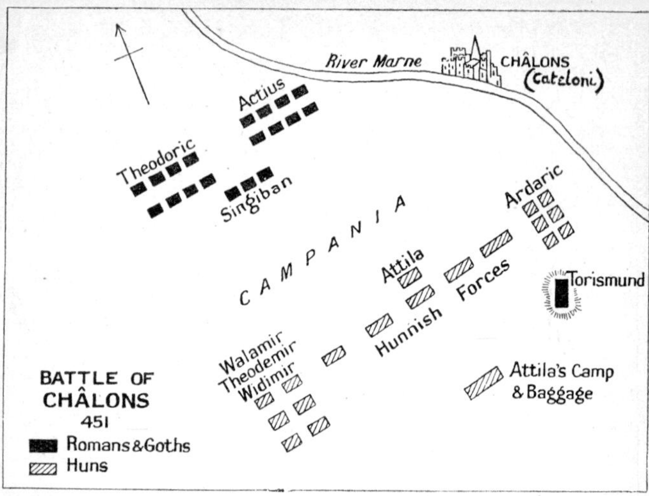

See Gibbon's "Decline and Fall of the Roman Empire." Creasy's "Fifteen Decisive Battles of the World," etc., etc.

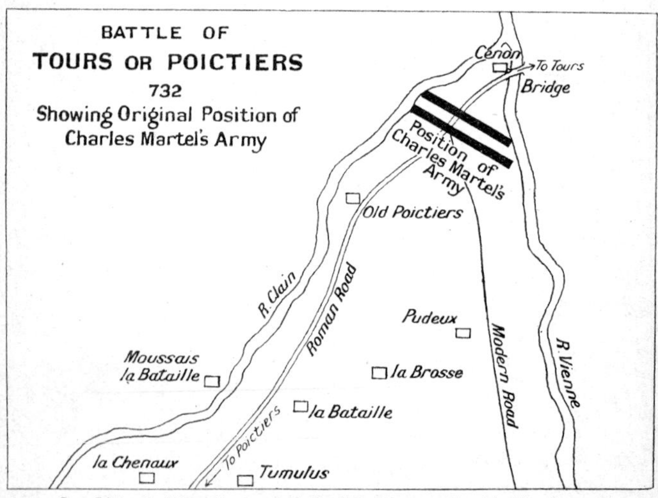

See Gibbon's "Decline and Fall of the Roman Empire." Creasy's "Fifteen Decisive Battles of the World," etc., etc.

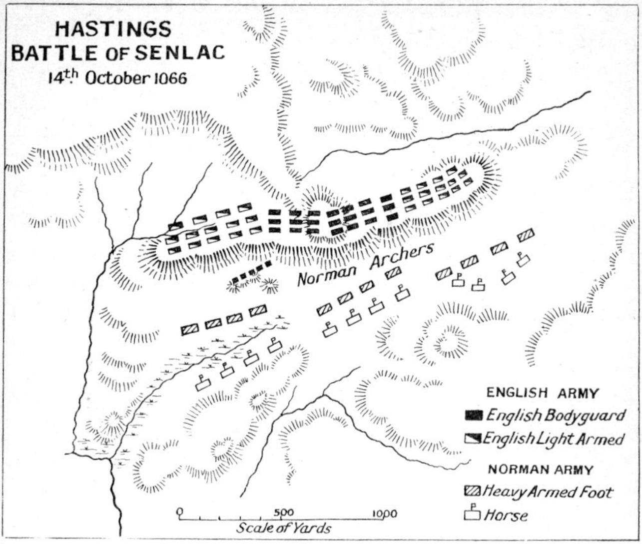

HASTINGS
BATTLE OF SENLAC
14th October 1066
Norman Archers
ENGLISH ARMY
English Bodyguard
English Light Armed
NORMAN ARMY
Heavy Armed Foot
Horse
0
500
1000
Scale of Yards

See Thierry's "Norman Conquest." Lytton's "Harold." Creasy's "Fifteen Decisive Battles of the World," etc., etc.

ORLEANS
BEFORE
JOAN OF ARC'S
ENTRY
St. Jean de la Ruelle
To Artenay & Paris
To Fleury
To Boigny
La Grande Espere
Bridge
St. Loup
St. Marc
St. Madeline
Orleans
River
Loire
To Croix
Montision
Works constructed by English
English Camp

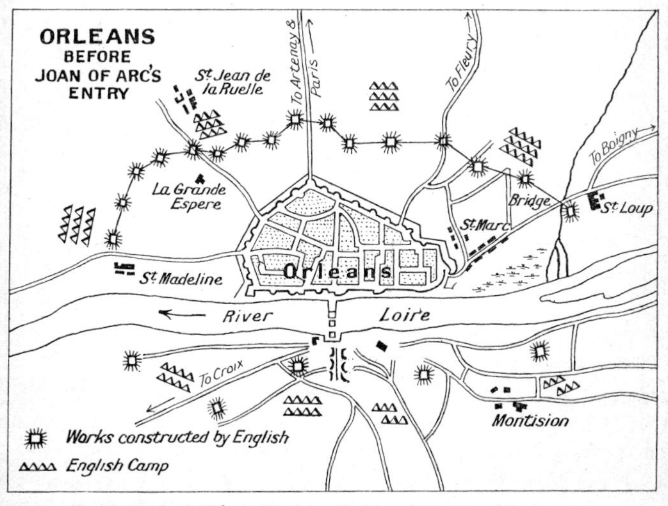

See Creasy's "Fifteen Decisive Battles of the World," etc., etc.

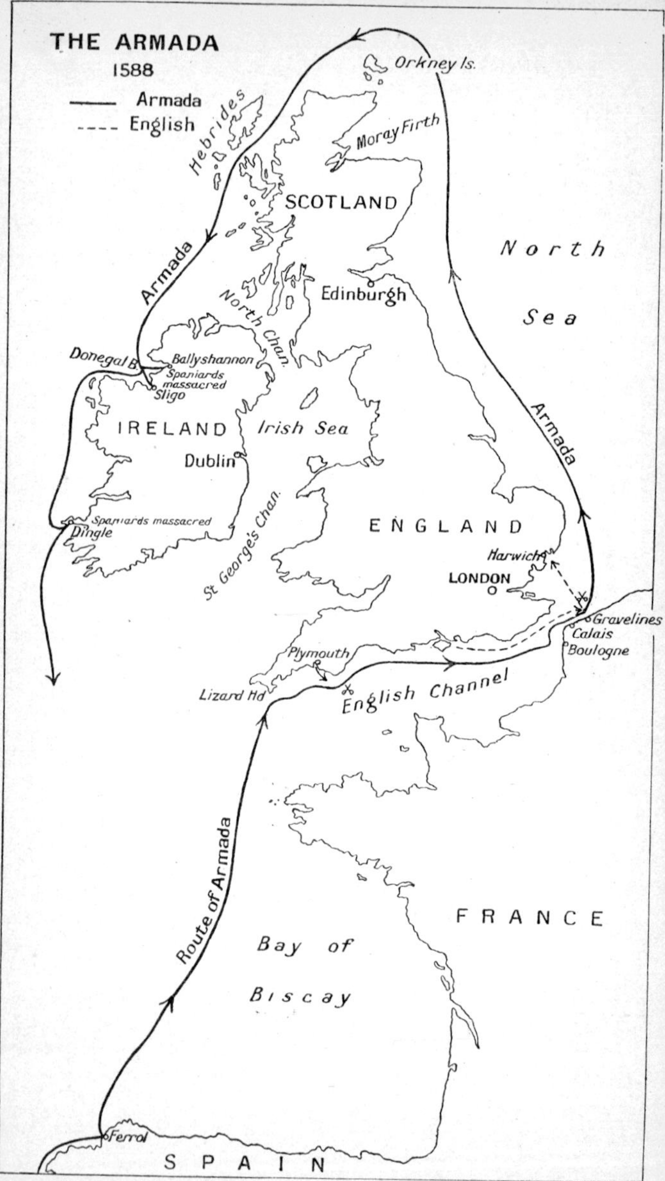

See Strickland's "Life of Queen Elizabeth." Kingsley's "Westward Ho!" Creasy's "Fifteen Decisive Battles of the World," etc., etc.

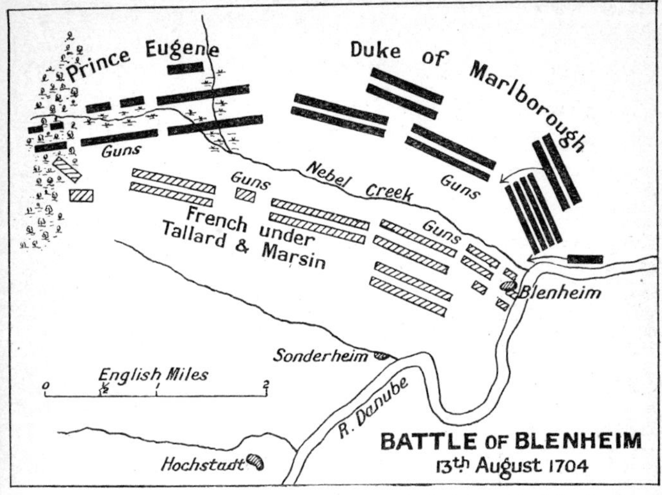

See Thackeray's "Henry Esmond." Creasy's "Fifteen Decisive Battles of the World," etc., etc.

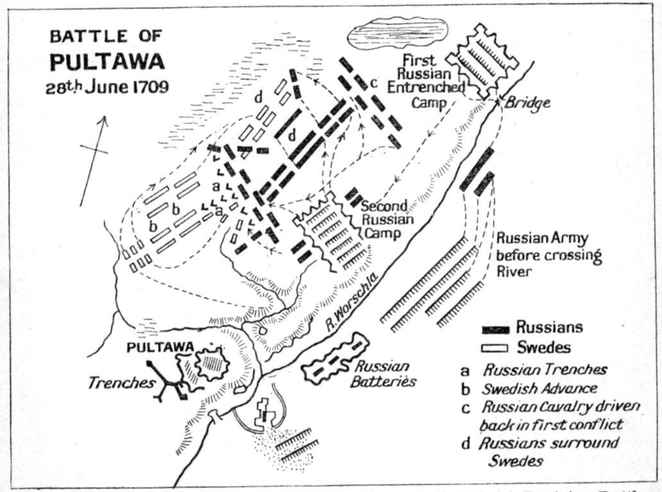

See Voltaire's "Life of Charles XII." Creasy's "Fifteen Decisive Battles of the World," etc., etc.

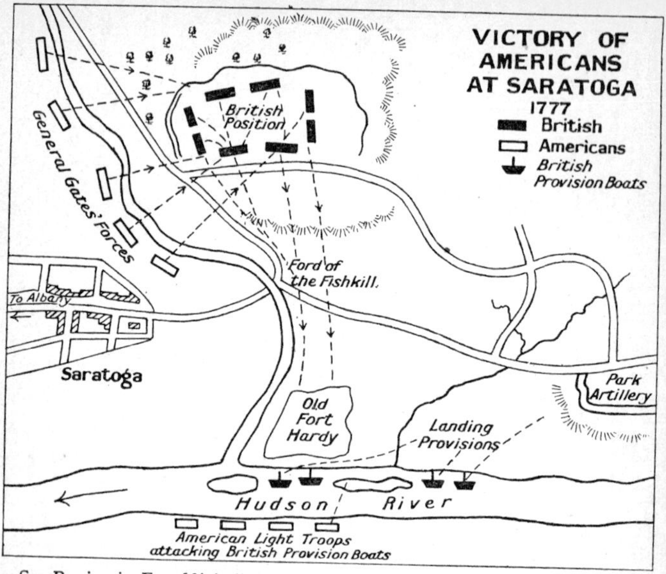

VICTORY OF AMERICANS AT SARATOGA
1777
British
Americans
British Provision Boats
British Position
General Gates' Forces
Ford of the Fishkill.
To Albany
Saratoga
Old Fort Hardy
Park Artillery
Landing Provisions
Hudson River
American Light Troops attacking British Provision Boats

See Benjamin Franklin's "Autobiography." Creasy's "Fifteen Decisive Battles of the World," etc., etc.

BATTLE OF VALMY
20th September 1792
Hans
Maffrecourt
Somme Bionne
Valmy
Braux
To St. Menehould
Donmartin
Dampierre
To Châlons
Gizacourt
R. Auve
Vailemont
Felcourt
R. Yevre
To Vitry
Prussians & Austrians
French

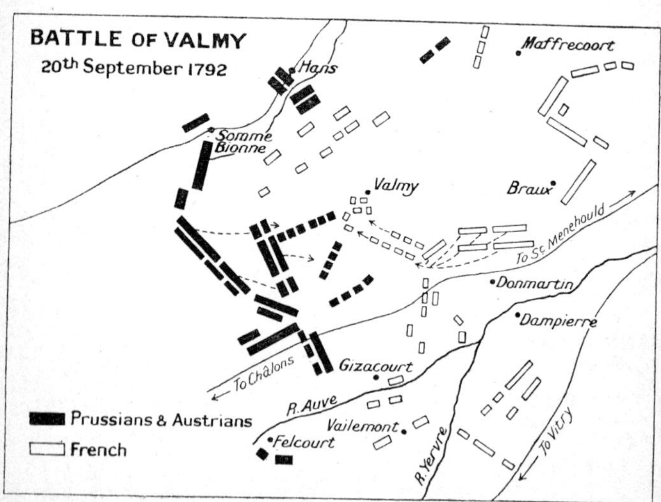

See Creasy's "Fifteen Decisive Battles of the World," etc., etc.

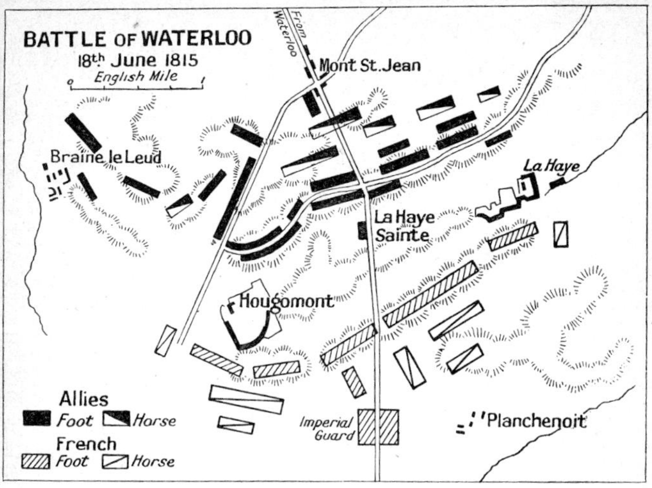

See Gleig's "Life of Wellington." Creasy's "Fifteen Decisive Battles of the World," etc., etc.

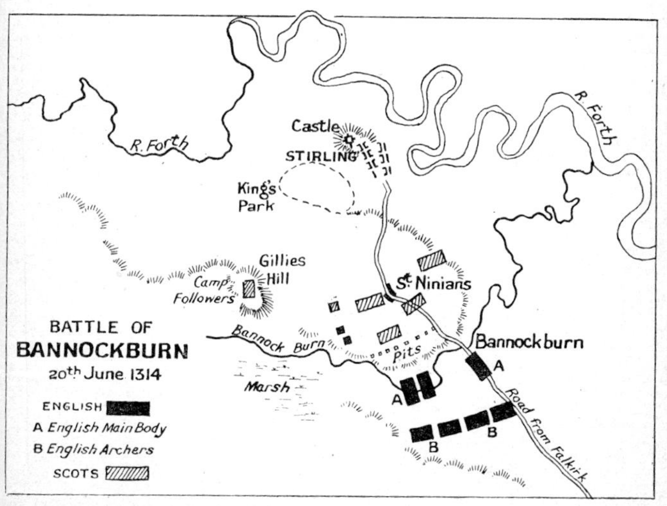

See Porter's "Scottish Chiefs," etc., etc.

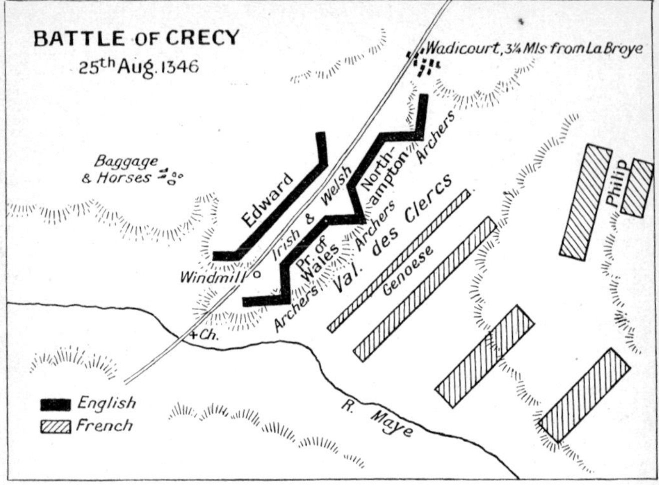

See J. G. Edgar's "Cressy and Poictiers," etc., etc.

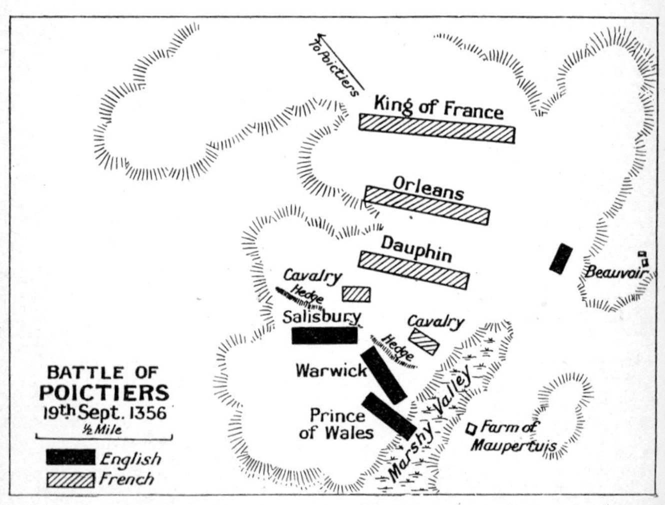

See J. G. Edgar's "Cressy and Poictiers," etc., etc.

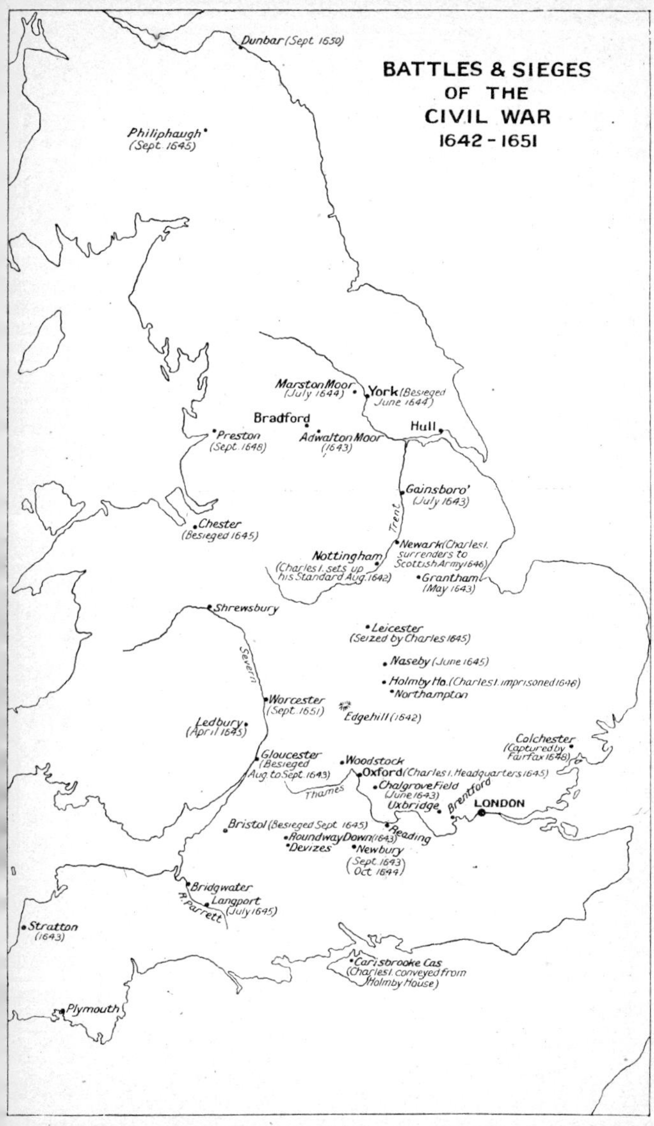

See Carlyle's " Cromwell's Letters and Speeches." " Col. Hutchinson's Memoirs." Scott's " Woodstock," etc., etc.

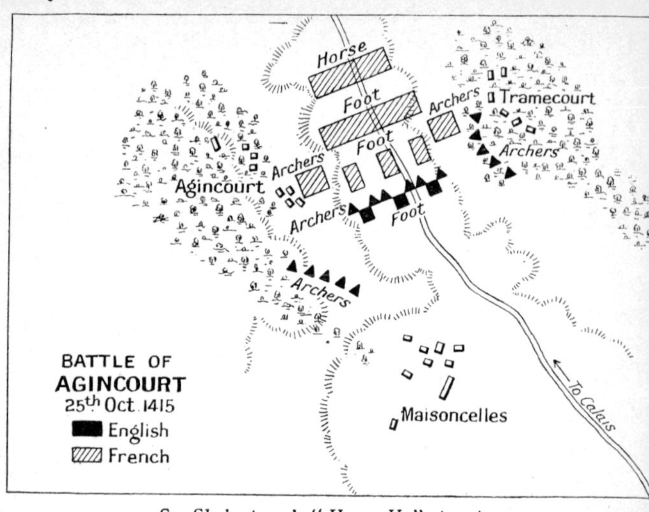

See Shakespeare's "Henry V.," etc., etc.

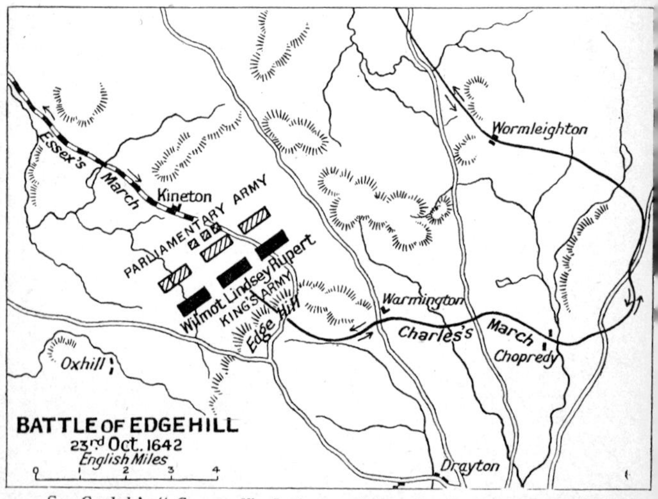

See Carlyle's "Cromwell's Letters and Speeches." "Col. Hutchinson's Memoirs," etc., etc.

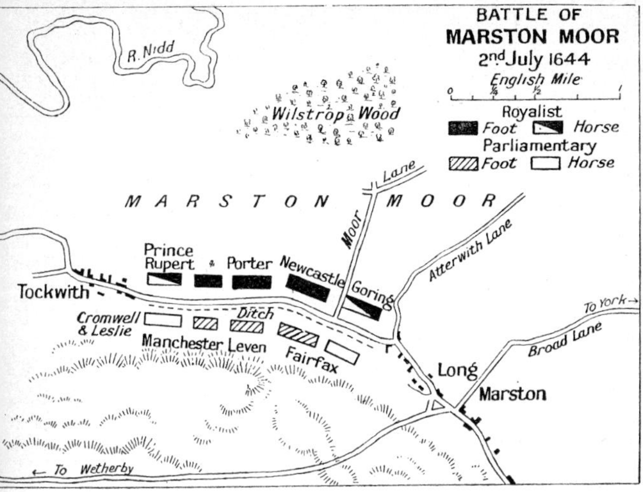

See Carlyle's "Cromwell's Letters and Speeches." "Col. Hutchinson's Memoirs," etc., etc.

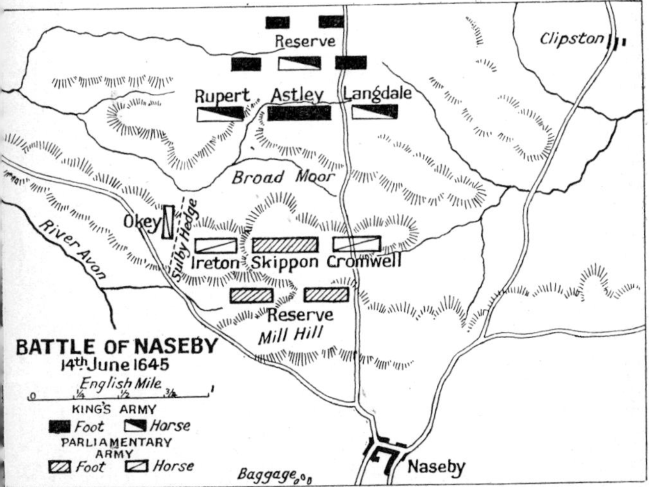

See Carlyle's "Cromwell's Letters and Speeches." "Col. Hutchinson's Memoirs," etc., etc.

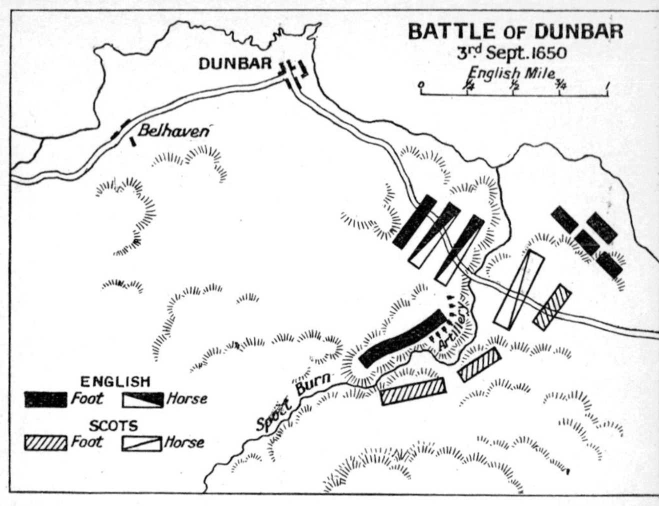

See Carlyle's "Cromwell's Letters and Speeches." "Col. Hutchinson's Memoirs," etc., etc.

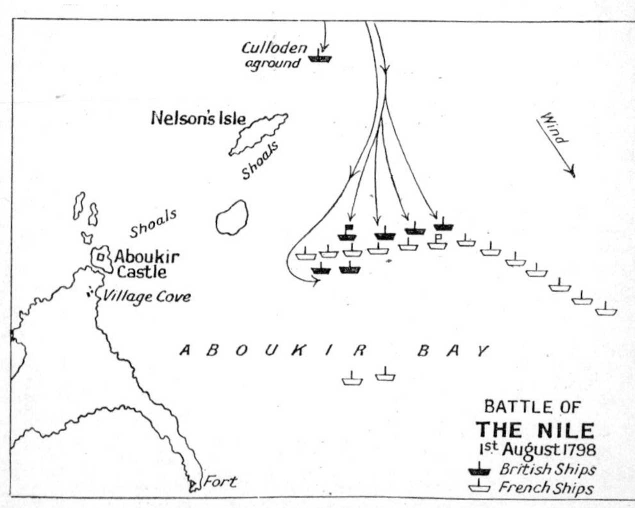

See Southey's "Life of Nelson," etc., etc.

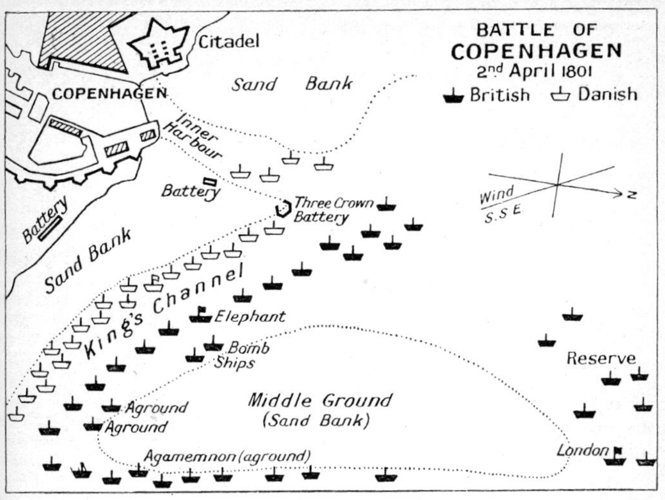

See Southey's "Life of Nelson," etc., etc.

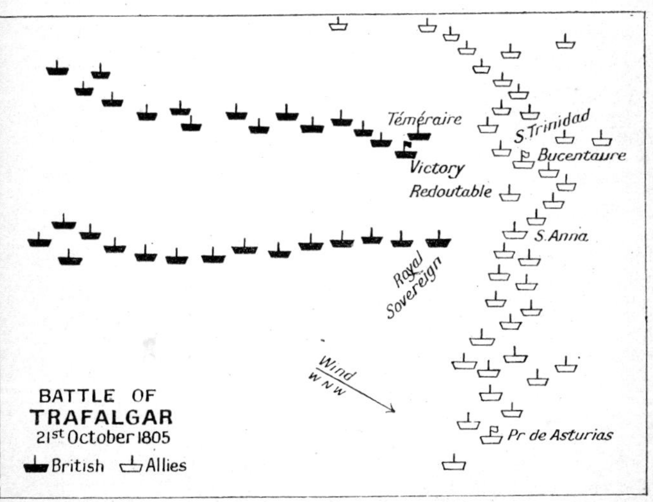

See Southey's "Life of Nelson," etc., etc

LONDON
Tabard Inn. Southwark
Watering of St Thomas
Deptford (Depeford)
Greenwich
Crayford
Dartford
Gravesend
Strood
Rochester
River Thames
R. Medway
Isle of Sheppey
Rainham
Watling Street
Sittingbourne (Sidingborne)
Ospringe
Faversham
Boughton (Boughton-under Blee)
Harbledown (? Bob-up-and-Down)
Blean
CANTERBURY
ROUTE OF THE
CANTERBURY
PILGRIMS
from
London to Canterbury

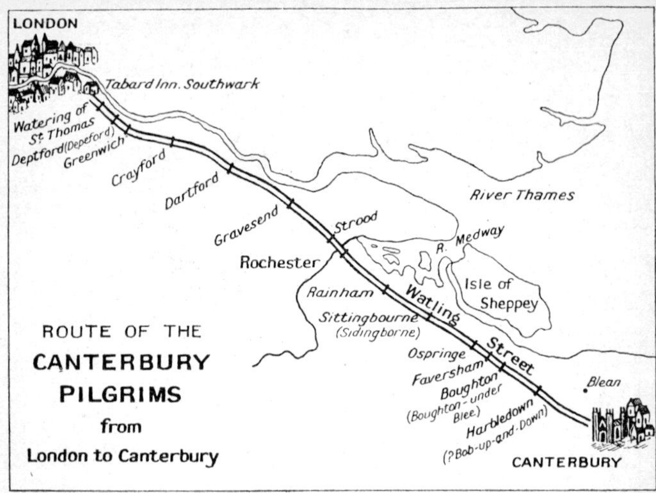

This shows only one of the pilgrims' routes to Canterbury, probably the one mentioned by Chaucer in his " Canterbury Tales." See also Stanley's " Memorials of Canterbury," etc., etc.

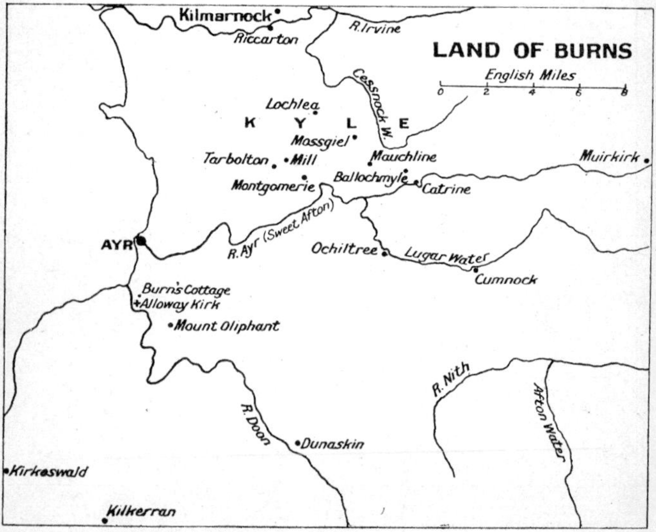

LAND OF BURNS
English Miles
0 2 4 6 8
Kilmarnock
Riccarton
R. Irvine
Cessnock W.
Lochlea
K Y L E
Mossgiel
Tarbolton
Mill
Mauchline
Muirkirk
Montgomerie
Ballochmyle
Catrine
AYR
R. Ayr (Sweet Afton)
Ochiltree
Lugar Water
Cumnock
Burns Cottage
Alloway Kirk
Mount Oliphant
R. Nith
Afton Water
R. Doon
Dunaskin
Kirkoswald
Kilkerran

See Lockhart's " Life of Robert Burns," etc., etc.